ideals

Low Calorie COOKBOOK

by Darlene Kronschnabel

Ideals Publishing Corp.

Milwaukee, Wisconsin

Introduction

Today most of us count calories. It's the commonsense way to a healthy life. *Ideals Low Calorie Cookbook* provides you with a wide variety of delicious recipes all based on a light approach to eating. These recipes strip away extra calories by using lean meats, poultry, fish, fresh fruits, and vegetables. Family favorites can still be on the menu, but with surprisingly fewer calories.

Best-selling author Darlene Kronschnabel presents some of the tastiest low-calorie recipes to be found, such as Julienne Beef Garden Salad, Rock Lobster Continental, German-Style Green Beans, and Chocolate Cloud. To aid those keeping track of total caloric intake, each recipe gives the approximate calorie content per serving.

Guided by the *Low Calorie Cookbook,* you can prepare delicious, sensible and satisfying meals while trimming calories at the same time.

A very special thank you to the following for their cooperation and help in supplying selected recipes: American Egg Board, American Lamb Council, American Spice Trade Association, Angostura International Limited, Apricot Advisory Board, Beatrice Foods, California Grape Commission, California Honey Advisory Board, California Iceberg Lettuce Commission, California Tree Fruit Agreement, Campbell Soup, Castle & Cooke Foods/Dole, Del Monte Kitchens, Durkee Foods, Florida Celery Commission, Florida Lime Commission, Fleischmann Yeast, General Foods Consumer Center, General Mills, Inc., Hunt-Wessons, Mushroom Institute, La Choy Food Products, Libby, McNeil & Libby, Livestock & Meat Board, Beef Industry Council, Kellogg's Company, International Apple Institute, National Broiler Council, National Kraut Packers Association, Oklahoma Peanut Commission, Ralston Purina Co., Rice Council of America, R. T. French, South African Lobster Service Corporation, Stokely Van Camp, Sunkist Growers, Thomas J. Lipton, Inc., Turkey Information Service., Tuna Research Foundation, United Dairy Association, United Fresh Fruit & Vegetable, Washington State Apple Commission, Western Iceberg Lettuce, Wisconsin Department of Agriculture, Wheat Flour Institute.

ISBN 0-8249-3003-7

Copyright © MCMLXXXI by Darlene Kronschnabel

All rights reserved.

Printed and bound in the United States of America.

Published by Ideals Publishing Corporation

11315 Watertown Plank Road

Milwaukee, WI 53226

Published simultaneously in Canada.

Cover recipes
Rock Lobster Vegetable Salad, 15
Apricot Chicken, 32
Grapefruit Velvet Fluff, 12

Cookbook Editor
Julie Hogan

Below is a listing of some common foods which are called for in this book.

Approx. Calories

Fruit Juice, 8 ounces
Apple 120
Orange, fresh 110
Tomato 45

Grain Products, 1 cup
Macaroni, cooked 155
Noodles, egg, cooked 200
Noodles, chow mein 211
Rice, enriched, regular . . 225
Rice, brown, cooked 272
Spaghetti, cooked 155

Cheeses, 1 ounce
American, blue, Roquefort,
Swiss 105
Cheddar 115
Cottage, creamed 30
Cream 106

Creamer, 1 teaspoon
Powdered, nondairy, ... 10

Creams, 1 ounce
Half and half 40
Whipping, unwhipped 89
Sour 60

Milk, 8 ounces
Nonfat, reconstituted skim 80
Skim, fortified 90
Whole 160
1% 110

Yogurt, 8 ounces
Plain 150
With fruit 260

Fats and Oils, 1 tablespoon
Butter, margarine 100
Oil (corn, olive, peanut,
safflower, salad) 125

Salad Dressings, 1 tablespoon
Blue cheese 75
French 65
Mayonnaise 100
Thousand Island 80

Contents

Appetizers and Beverages 4

Soups and Stews 6

Salads 11

Vegetables 18

Beef 22

Poultry 31

Pork, Veal, Lamb 38

Seafood 43

Eggs and Cheese 50

Breads 54

Desserts 59

Index 64

Appetizers and Beverages

Be sure to count the nibbles and drinks enjoyed during social events and throughout the day as part of a day's calorie allotment.

Miniature Meatballs

Makes 24.
Approximately 38 calories each.

 1 pound lean ground beef
 1 teaspoon salt
   Dash black pepper
24 pretzel sticks

Preheat oven to 325°. Combine beef, salt, and pepper. Shape into balls, using 1 tablespoon seasoned ground beef for each ball. Place in a shallow baking dish. Bake for 15 to 20 minutes. Insert a pretzel stick into each ball. Serve hot with Zippy Sauce (Recipe below).

Vegetable Sticks

Makes 8 cups.
Approximately 43 calories per ½-cup serving.

 1 pound fresh green beans, trimmed
 1 pound carrots, peeled and cut into thin sticks
 3 teaspoons dried dillweed
 2 teaspoons mustard seed
 4 cloves garlic, halved
2½ cups water
 1 cup cider vinegar
 ½ cup sugar

Cook beans and carrots separately in boiling, salted water until tender-crisp; drain. Combine beans, carrots, dillweed, mustard seed, and garlic in a covered container. In a small saucepan, combine water, vinegar, and sugar. Bring to a boil. Pour marinade over vegetables. Cool. Cover and chill overnight. Vegetables may be stored up to 2 weeks in refrigerator.

Zippy Sauce

Makes 1 cup.
Approximately 161 calories per cup; 10 calories per tablespoon.

 1 cup catsup
 2 tablespoons prepared horseradish

Combine catsup and horseradish and blend well. Serve hot or cold.

Grapefruit-Ham Roll-Ups

Makes 32 appetizers.
Approximately 29 calories each.

 1 3-ounce package imitation cream cheese, softened
 2 tablespoons minced green onion
 1 tablespoon sesame seed, toasted
1½ teaspoons grated lemon peel
 1 teaspoon grated grapefruit peel
 8 square slices ham (about 8 ounces)
 2 grapefruit, peeled and sectioned
   Sliced olives, optional

Combine cream cheese, onion, sesame seed, lemon, and grapefruit peel; stir until smooth. Spread each slice of ham with about 1 tablespoon cream cheese mixture. Place 2 grapefruit sections on 1 end of each ham slice; roll up. Secure with a toothpick; cut each roll into fourths. Garnish with sliced olives.

Beef and Pearls

Makes 16 servings.
Approximately 54 calories per serving.

 1 pound lean ground beef
 1 teaspoon salt
   Dash black pepper
32 small pickled onions

Preheat oven to 325°. Combine beef, salt, and pepper. Shape into balls, using about 2 teaspoons seasoned ground beef for each. Alternate 2 balls and 2 onions on each of 16 wooden skewers. Place in a shallow baking dish. Bake in a slow oven for 15 to 20 minutes. Serve hot with Zippy Sauce (Recipe below).

Vegetable Dip for Apples

Makes 2½ cups.
Approximately 44 calories per ¼-cup serving.

¼ cup sour cream
 2 cups low-fat plain yogurt
¼ cup grated carrot
 2 tablespoons chopped parsley
 6 radishes, thinly sliced

Combine sour cream with yogurt. Add carrot, parsley, and radishes; mix well. Serve as dip with Delicious apples.

Pickled Mushrooms

Makes 6 servings.
Approximately 41 calories per serving.

  ½ pound fresh mushrooms
  2 teaspoons salt
  2 cups boiling water
  ⅓ cup wine vinegar
  ⅓ cup cider vinegar
  1 small onion, sliced
  6 black peppercorns
  ¼ teaspoon tarragon
  ¼ teaspoon celery seed
  1 tablespoon vegetable oil

Clean mushrooms; cut stems even with the cap. Leave button mushrooms whole. Slice larger mushrooms in halves or quarters. Add mushrooms to salted, boiling water. Simmer for 5 minutes; drain. In a small saucepan, combine vinegars, onion, and seasonings. Bring the mixture to a boil and cook for 10 minutes. Add oil. Remove from heat and cool. Combine mushrooms and marinade in a medium-size bowl; mix well. Cover tightly and refrigerate at least 1 day before using. Drain well and serve.

Trim Toddy

Makes 6 servings.
Approximately 22 calories per serving.

  1 24-ounce can vegetable juice cocktail
  1 cup tea
  ⅛ teaspoon cinnamon
    Orange slices

Combine vegetable juice cocktail, tea, and cinnamon in a saucepan. Heat; stir occasionally. Serve in mugs garnished with orange slices.

Orange Nog

Makes 4 servings.
Approximately 80 calories per serving.

  2 cups skim milk
  2 teaspoons granulated sugar
  1 cup crushed ice
  1 cup fresh orange juice
  2 teaspoons grated orange rind

Place milk, sugar, and ice in a shaker or fruit jar; shake well. Add orange juice and rind and shake vigorously. (If orange juice is very tart, more sugar may be needed.)

Fruited Punch

Makes 25 5-ounce servings.
Approximately 49 calories per serving.

  2 1.8-ounce envelopes or ½ cup lemon-flavored iced tea mix
  4 cups fresh orange juice
  1 cup water
  2 cups blueberries
  3 peaches, peeled and thinly sliced
  2 bananas, thinly sliced
  1 8-ounce jar maraschino cherries, cut in half, reserve syrup
  1 28-ounce bottle club soda, chilled

In a punch bowl, combine iced tea mix, orange juice, and water. Add blueberries, peaches, bananas, cherries, and reserved syrup; chill. Just before serving, add club soda.

Niced Tea

Makes 2 servings.
Approximately 35 calories per serving.

  1 12-ounce can vegetable juice cocktail, chilled
  1 cup prepared instant lemon-flavored iced tea
  2 lime wedges

Combine all ingredients in a pitcher.

Root Beer Float

Makes 1 serving.
Approximately 64 calories per serving.

  1 12-ounce can low-calorie root beer
  ¼ cup vanilla ice cream

Fill a tall beverage glass ⅔ full of root beer; add ice cream.

Sweetheart Punch

Makes 24 servings.
Approximately 2 calories per serving.

  2 quarts low-calorie cherry soda
  1 quart low-calorie orange soda
  1 quart low-calorie lemon-lime soda
  1 orange or lemon, thinly sliced

Freeze 1 quart cherry soda for beverage cubes. Chill remaining soft drinks. When ready to serve, shave or crack beverage cubes; place in punch bowl. Add other soft drinks slowly. Garnish with orange or lemon slices.

Soups and Stews

Garden Ring Soup

Makes 8 servings.

Approximately 74 calories per serving.

- 1 15½-ounce can cut green beans, drained, reserve liquid
- 1 15-ounce can cut asparagus, drained, reserve liquid
- 1 cup celery chunks (about 1-inch pieces)
- 2 cups chicken broth
- 1 teaspoon Worcestershire sauce
- ¾ cup enriched durum macaroni rings
  Snipped parsley
- 1 lemon, sliced

Combine liquids from beans and asparagus to make 1 cup. Place vegetables and celery with the reserved juice in a blender container; puree. In a medium saucepan, bring chicken broth and Worcestershire sauce to a boil. Add macaroni and cook until tender, yet firm, about 4 minutes. Add pureed vegetables and heat through. Garnish with parsley and lemon slices.

Tropical Soup

Makes 4 servings.

Approximately 106 calories per serving.

- 1 10¾-ounce can condensed cream of chicken soup
- 1 soup can skim milk
- 1 teaspoon lime juice
- ½ cup mashed, ripe banana
- ½ cup seedless grapes, halved
  Grated lime rind
  Ground nutmeg

Combine soup, milk, and lime juice in a saucepan. Blend thoroughly. Heat through, stirring occasionally. Chill for at least 6 hours. Before serving, blend in banana and grapes. Garnish with lime rind and nutmeg.

Penny-Pinching Pot

Makes 1½ quarts soup.

Approximately 132 calories per 1-cup serving.

- 1 tablespoon vegetable oil
- 4 cups thinly sliced celery
- 2 cloves garlic, minced
- 1 envelope onion soup mix
- 2 cups water
- 1 1-pound can whole tomatoes, drained and chopped, reserve liquid
- 1 20-ounce can white or red kidney beans, drained

Heat oil in a large saucepan. Add celery and garlic and sauté for 5 minutes. Combine onion soup and water. Add tomatoes, reserved tomato liquid, and onion soup mixture to celery. Cook, covered, 20 minutes, stirring occasionally. Add beans and cook 10 minutes.

Hamburger Soup

Makes 6 servings.

Approximately 177 calories per serving.

- 1 pound lean ground beef
- 1 cup diced onion
- ½ cup cubed raw potatoes
- 1 cup sliced carrots
- ½ cup diced celery
- 1 cup shredded cabbage
- 1 8-ounce can tomato sauce
- ¼ cup raw rice
- 1 small bay leaf, crushed
- ½ teaspoon thyme
- 1 leaf sweet basil
- 4 teaspoons salt
  Dash black pepper
- 1½ quarts water

Place hamburger and onion in a large kettle; brown meat. Drain fat. Add potatoes, carrots, celery, cabbage, and tomato sauce. Bring to a boil. Sprinkle rice into mixture. Add remaining ingredients. Cover and simmer for 1 hour.

Asparagus Soup

Makes 4 servings.

Approximately 64 calories per serving.

- ¾ cup water
- ¾ teaspoon salt
- 1 pound fresh asparagus, cut into pieces (about 2½ cups)
- 1 cup skim milk
- 1 tablespoon margarine
  Parsley flakes, optional

In a saucepan, heat water and salt to boiling. Add asparagus; cover and simmer 8 to 10 minutes, until asparagus is just tender. Place asparagus and cooking water into a blender container; cover and blend on low speed until asparagus is finely chopped. Add milk; blend on high speed until smooth. Return soup to saucepan; add margarine and heat through. If desired, dot each serving with parsley flakes.

Sauerkraut Soup

Makes 12 servings.
Approximately 86 calories per serving.

- 1 pound beef short ribs
- ½ cup chopped onion
- 1 30-ounce can sauerkraut
- 6 cups fat-skimmed beef stock
- 1 1-pound can whole tomatoes
- 10 peppercorns
- 2 bay leaves
  Salt to taste

Trim fat from short ribs. Brown onion and short ribs in a nonstick frying pan over medium heat. Add sauerkraut and toss lightly. Add remaining ingredients. Bring to a boil, reduce heat, and simmer for 40 minutes. Remove short ribs, peppercorns, and bay leaves. Cut meat from the bones; cut into chunks and return to soup. Correct seasonings.

Tuna Stew

Makes 6 servings.
Approximately 151 calories per serving.

- 4 cups chicken broth
- 2 cups water
- 2 medium potatoes, pared and diced
- 1 small onion, thinly sliced
- 2 tablespoons chopped celery leaves
- 1 teaspoon salt
- 3 whole peppercorns
- ¾ teaspoon crushed marjoram
- 1 10-ounce package frozen spinach, thawed and drained
- 2 6½- or 7-ounce cans tuna, packed in water, drained and flaked

Combine chicken broth, water, potatoes, onion, celery leaves, salt, and peppercorns in a large kettle. Bring to a boil. Reduce heat and simmer 10 minutes, until potatoes are tender. Add marjoram, spinach, and tuna; simmer 5 minutes.

Camper's Stew

Makes 6 servings.
Approximately 208 calories per serving.

- 1 pound lean ground beef
- ¼ cup chopped onion
- 1 teaspoon salt
- ½ teaspoon chili powder
- 1 28-ounce can tomatoes with liquid, broken up
- 1½ cups bite-size crispy wheat squares
- 1 cup cubed, cooked potatoes or 1 8-ounce can potatoes, drained
- 2 8-ounce cans mixed vegetables, undrained

Brown ground beef and onion in a frying pan until onion is tender. Drain fat, if necessary. Stir in salt and chili powder. Add tomatoes and liquid and wheat squares. Bring to a boil; reduce heat, cover and simmer 8 to 10 minutes. Stir occasionally. Add remaining ingredients. Simmer 5 minutes.

Vegetable Stew

Makes 8 servings.
Approximately 64 calories per serving.

- 2 potatoes, pared and cubed
- 2 carrots, pared and sliced
- ½ head cauliflower, broken into flowerets
- 2 ribs celery, sliced
- ½ pound mushrooms, sliced
- 2 onions, sliced
- 1 sweet red pepper, cut into strips
- 1 clove garlic, minced
- 1 13¾-ounce can chicken broth
- 2 teaspoons salt
  Dash black pepper
- 2 tablespoons chopped fresh dill or 2 teaspoons dried dillweed

Preheat oven to 350°. Combine all ingredients in a 3-quart baking dish. Cover and bake for 1 hour or until the vegetables are tender.

Fish Stew

Makes 6 servings.
Approximately 208 calories per serving.

- 2 teaspoons vegetable oil
- ½ cup chopped onion
- 1 clove garlic, minced
- 1 28-ounce can tomatoes, broken up
- 1 12-ounce bottle clam juice
- 1 teaspoon salt
- 1 teaspoon crushed oregano
- ¼ teaspoon black pepper
- 1½ pounds fresh or frozen halibut or cod steaks
- 1 pound fresh mushrooms, sliced or 2 8-ounce cans sliced mushrooms, drained
- 1 10-ounce can baby clams, undrained
- ¼ cup chopped parsley

Heat oil in a Dutch oven or a large saucepan. Add onion and garlic; sauté for 2 minutes. Add tomatoes, clam juice, salt, oregano, and pepper. Bring to a boil. Reduce heat, cover, and simmer, for 30 minutes. Cut fish into 1-inch chunks, discarding bones. Add mushrooms, fish, and clams to Dutch oven. Return to a boil. Reduce heat and simmer, covered, until fish flakes easily, about 10 minutes. Garnish with parsley.

Beef and Celery Stew

Makes 8 servings.
Approximately 220 calories per serving.

- 1 whole stalk celery
- 2½ pounds lean beef stew meat
- 2 cups water
- 2 beef bouillon cubes
- ¼ teaspoon instant minced garlic
- 1 teaspoon thyme leaves
- 1 teaspoon salt
  Dash black pepper
- 4 sprigs parsley
- ½ pound fresh mushrooms, sliced
- ½ pound small white onions

Trim ends of celery; reserve leaves. Slice celery into 1-inch pieces; set aside. (Makes about 6 cups.) Arrange beef on a rack in a broiler pan. Broil, 4 inches from heat source, 15 to 20 minutes, turning to brown all sides. Transfer beef to a large, heavy saucepan or Dutch oven. Add water, bouillon, garlic, thyme, salt, and pepper; mix well. Use string to tie together parsley and reserved celery leaves. Add to saucepan. Bring to a boil. Reduce heat and simmer, covered, for 1½ hours. Add mushrooms, onions, and reserved celery; simmer until meat and vegetables are tender, about 30 minutes. Remove celery leaves and parsley before serving.

Chicken and Vegetable Stew

Makes 6 servings.
Approximately 177 calories per serving.

- 2 whole chicken breasts, split, skinned, boned and cut into 2-inch pieces (1 pound boneless)
- 2 10¾-ounce cans condensed chicken broth
- ½ cup raw rice
- ½ cup sherry
- 2 tablespoons soy sauce
- 1 large clove garlic, minced
- ¼ teaspoon ground ginger
- 2 cups diagonally sliced carrots
- 1 cup diagonally sliced green onion
- 1 8-ounce can sliced bamboo shoots, drained
- 1 6-ounce package frozen pea pods

Lightly brown chicken over medium heat in a nonstick frying pan. Add broth, rice, sherry, soy sauce, garlic, and ginger. Bring to a boil. Reduce heat, cover, and simmer for 15 minutes. Add carrots, onion, and bamboo shoots. Simmer 5 minutes or until carrots are tender. Stir occasionally. Add pea pods and heat thoroughly.

Mulligan Stew

Makes 6 servings.
Approximately 231 calories per serving.

- 1 tablespoon vegetable oil
- 3 medium onions, sliced
- 1½ pounds fresh or frozen fish fillets such as cod or halibut, thawed
- 1 quart boiling water
- 3 large carrots, pared and diced
- 1 6-ounce can tomato paste
- 1½ pounds potatoes, pared and cubed
- ½ cup diced celery, including leaves
- 4 teaspoons salt
- ¼ teaspoon black pepper

Heat oil in a heavy Dutch oven or kettle. Add onions and sauté until tender. Slice fish into 1-inch pieces. Add fish and remaining ingredients to onions. Cover and simmer 25 minutes or until vegetables are tender.

Double Mushroom and Beef Stew

Makes 8 servings.
Approximately 380 calories per serving.

- 2 pounds lean stewing beef, cut into 1½-inch cubes
- ¼ cup flour
- 1 tablespoon salt
- ¼ teaspoon black pepper
- 2 tablespoons vegetable oil
- 1 cup chopped onion
- 1 28-ounce can tomatoes, broken up
- 1 cup water
- 3 cups potatoes, cut into 2-inch chunks
- 2 cups cut green beans or 1 10-ounce package frozen, cut green beans
- 1 pound fresh mushrooms
- 3 tablespoons margarine

Place beef in a large bowl. Combine flour, salt, and black pepper; sprinkle over beef and toss lightly to coat. Heat oil in a large saucepan or a Dutch oven. Add beef cubes a few at a time and brown on all sides. Remove and set aside. Add onion and sauté for 2 minutes. Add tomatoes and water; stir and scrape drippings from bottom of pan. Add reserved beef cubes. Bring to a boil. Reduce heat and simmer, covered, for 1½ hours, stirring occasionally. Add potatoes; cover and simmer 30 minutes. Add green beans; cover and simmer 30 minutes, or until beef and vegetables are tender. Rinse, pat dry, and slice mushrooms. Melt margarine in a large skillet. Add mushrooms and sauté for 5 minutes. Stir into stew just before serving.

Slim Potato Salad

Makes 1 serving.
Approximately 113 calories per serving.

1 medium potato, boiled and diced
1 tablespoon chopped onion
1 tablespoon chopped celery
1 tablespoon chopped green pepper
1 tablespoon low-calorie French dressing
  Salt to taste
  Freshly ground black pepper

Combine all ingredients in a bowl; toss lightly.

Note: Potato salads made with mayonnaise, about 145 to 200 calories per serving.

Scandinavian Ham Salad

Makes 6 servings.
Approximately 156 calories per serving.

1 fresh pineapple
2 cups cubed, cooked ham
6 cherry tomatoes, halved
1 cup sliced celery
¼ cup sliced green onion
½ cup imitation sour cream
½ teaspoon dillweed
½ teaspoon hot mustard
¼ teaspoon salt
¼ teaspoon lemon juice
⅛ teaspoon garlic salt
  Dash black pepper

Cut pineapple in half lengthwise through crown. Remove pulp, leaving shells intact. Core and dice pulp. In a large bowl, combine pineapple, ham, tomatoes, celery, and onion. In a small bowl, combine remaining ingredients; mix well. Spoon dressing over pineapple mixture, tossing gently to mix. Spoon salad into pineapple shells.

Saucy Raspberry Apple Mold

Makes 6 servings.
Approximately 61 calories per serving.

1 3-ounce package low-calorie raspberry gelatin
1 cup boiling water
½ cup cold water
1 17-ounce can applesauce

Dissolve gelatin in the boiling water. Add remaining water. Chill until slightly thickened. Fold in applesauce. Pour into a 3-cup mold or 6 individual molds. Chill until set.

Oriental Chicken Salad

Makes 6 servings.
Approximately 109 calories per serving.

2 cups chopped, cooked chicken
1 cup bean sprouts
1 cup unsweetened pineapple chunks
½ cup sliced water chestnuts
¼ cup sliced celery
½ cup lite Russian dressing
  Shredded lettuce

In a medium bowl, combine all ingredients, except lettuce. Toss lightly. Chill. Serve on a bed of lettuce.

Sardine Salad

Makes 3 servings.
Approximately 142 calories per serving.

1 7½-ounce can sardines in tomato sauce, drained
  Lettuce
½ cup low-fat creamed cottage cheese

Fillet sardines. Arrange sardine fillets on lettuce-lined plate. Add a scoop of cottage cheese. Garnish with lemon wedges and parsley, if desired.

Celery Salad

Makes 8 servings.
Approximately 62 calories per serving.

1½ cups boiling water
3 tea bags
2 3-ounce packages low-calorie orange flavored gelatin
1 11-ounce can mandarin orange segments, drained, reserve liquid
1 8-ounce can pineapple chunks, drained, reserve liquid
4 teaspoons lemon juice
4 cups diced celery

Pour boiling water over tea bags; stir well. Let stand for 5 minutes. Remove tea bags. Pour hot tea over gelatin; stir to dissolve. Combine reserved fruit liquids. Add lemon juice and enough cold water to make 1½ cups liquid. Stir into gelatin mixture. Chill until mixture is as thick as unbeaten egg whites. Stir in oranges, pineapple, and celery. Pour into a 2-quart mold. Refrigerate until firm. Dip mold into hot water for a few seconds. Unmold onto a serving plate.

Chicken Dinner Salad

Makes 6 servings.
Approximately 88 calories per serving.

  1 head iceberg lettuce, cleaned and chilled
  1 16-ounce can cut green beans, drained
  1 apple, sliced
  2 cups cubed, cooked chicken

Cut lettuce into crosswise slices; then cut each slice into bite-size chunks. Place lettuce on a serving platter or in individual salad bowls. Arrange beans, apple, and chicken on lettuce. Serve with a favorite dressing.

Tossed Mushroom Salad

Makes 6 servings.
Approximately 40 calories per serving.

  ¼ pound fresh spinach
  ¼ head iceberg lettuce
  ½ pound fresh mushrooms, sliced
  8 cherry tomatoes, halved
  6 tablespoons plain low-fat yogurt
  2 tablespoons bottled low-calorie French dressing
  ¼ teaspoon crushed basil
  ⅛ teaspoon garlic powder

Tear spinach and lettuce into bite-size pieces and place in a salad bowl. Add mushrooms and tomatoes. Combine remaining ingredients and mix well. Pour over salad; toss gently.

Mandarin Peanut Mold

Makes 10 servings.
Approximately 98 calories per ½-cup serving.

  1 11-ounce can mandarin orange segments, drained, reserve liquid
  1 16-ounce can frozen concentrated orange juice, thawed
  1 3-ounce package low-calorie orange-flavored gelatin
  1 tablespoon minced candied ginger
  1 cup frozen nondairy whipped topping, thawed
  ½ cup cocktail peanuts, chopped

Combine reserved orange liquid and orange juice. Add enough water to measure 2 cups. Heat 1 cup of the liquid to boiling. Pour over gelatin, stirring until dissolved. Stir in ginger. Chill until partially thickened. Fold in whipped topping, oranges, and peanuts. Turn into a 5-cup ring mold. Chill until firm. To serve, unmold on lettuce. Center can be filled with tuna or chicken salad. Garnish with orange segments and peanuts.

Pea Salad

Makes 6 servings.
Approximately 137 calories per serving.

  1 17-ounce can peas, drained
  2 hard-cooked eggs, chopped
  ½ green pepper, chopped
  ½ cup chopped onion
  ¼ cup diced pasteurized process American cheese
  3 tablespoons reduced calorie mayonnaise
  ¼ teaspoon black pepper
  3 slices cooked bacon, crumbled

Combine the first 5 ingredients in a serving dish. Fold in mayonnaise and pepper. Sprinkle on bacon. Chill several hours before serving.

Orange and Onion Salad

Makes 4 servings.
Approximately 122 calories per serving.

  1 large Bermuda onion, cut into 8 thin slices
  2 large oranges, peeled and cut into 6 slices each
  ¼ teaspoon salt
  ⅛ teaspoon crushed oregano
  2 tablespoons vegetable oil
  1 tablespoon fresh orange juice
  1 tablespoon fresh lemon juice
  2 tablespoons sliced ripe olives
    Freshly ground black pepper

Place onion and oranges in a glass dish; combine salt, oregano, oil, orange, and lemon juice. Pour over onion and oranges; marinate for 15 minutes. Arrange oranges and onion on beds of crisp lettuce, alternating 3 orange slices and 2 onion slices per serving. Top with olives and spoon on marinade. Add a generous sprinkling of pepper.

Grapefruit Velvet Fluff

Makes 6 to 8 servings.
Approximately 79 calories per serving.

  1 3-ounce package low-calorie lime-flavored gelatin
  2 tablespoons sugar
  1 cup boiling water
  1 16-ounce can grapefruit sections, drained and diced, reserve liquid
  2 cups nondairy whipped topping

Dissolve gelatin and sugar in boiling water. Add enough water to reserved grapefruit liquid to make 1 cup liquid; stir into gelatin mixture. Chill until slightly thickened. Fold whipped topping into gelatin. Fold in grapefruit. Spoon into 6 or 8 individual dishes and chill until firm.

Lettuce and Radish Slaw

Makes 8 servings.
Approximately 46 calories per serving.

- ½ cup imitation sour cream
- ½ cup reduced calorie mayonnaise
- 2 tablespoons chopped onion
- 1 tablespoon fresh lemon juice
- ½ teaspoon salt
- ¼ teaspoon black pepper
- 1 tablespoon minced dill
- 1 large head iceberg lettuce, shredded
- 2 cups sliced radishes

Combine sour cream, mayonnaise, onion, lemon juice, salt, pepper, and dill in a small jar. Cover and shake. Chill. Combine lettuce and radishes in a large bowl. Drizzle on dressing and toss lightly.

Lettuce and Tomato Salad

Makes 8 servings.
Approximately 73 calories per serving.

- 1 cup reduced calorie mayonnaise
- 1 cup diced cucumber
- 1 tablespoon chopped onion
- 1 tablespoon minced parsley
- 3 tablespoons fresh lemon juice
  Dash black pepper
- 1 large head lettuce, torn into bite-size pieces
- 4 large tomatoes, cut into wedges

In a large bowl, combine mayonnaise, cucumber, onion, parsley, lemon juice, and pepper. Cover and chill until ready to use. Place lettuce in a salad bowl. Add tomatoes. Spoon dressing over salad; toss lightly.

Crisp 'n' Clear Orange Salad

Makes 6 servings.
Approximately 65 calories per serving.

- 1 head iceberg lettuce, cleaned and chilled
- 2 medium oranges, peeled
- ½ cup lite Italian dressing
- 2 to 3 tablespoons fresh lemon juice
- 1 red onion, thinly sliced and separated into rings
- 1 cucumber, peeled and sliced
- ½ cup minced parsley

Tear lettuce into bite-size pieces and place in a large salad bowl. Slice oranges into cartwheels; cut each in half. Mix Italian dressing with lemon juice. Add oranges, onion rings, cucumber, and parsley to lettuce; pour dressing over salad and toss lightly. Serve immediately.

Western Dessert Salad

Makes 4 servings.
Approximately 93 calories per serving.

- 1 small head iceberg lettuce, cleaned and chilled
  Dessert Salad Dressing (Recipe on page 16.)
- 1 large banana
- 1 medium orange, segmented
- 1 medium pink grapefruit, segmented
- ½ cup sliced strawberries

Shortly before serving, prepare Dessert Salad Dressing, using half of the banana. Slice remaining banana. Combine all fruit. Shred lettuce to measure 1 quart. Place ½ cup lettuce in the bottom of each of 4 serving bowls. Spoon ¼ cup fruit over each. Top with 2 tablespoons Dressing. Repeat layers.

Trim Tuna Salad

Makes 6 servings.
Approximately 158 calories per serving.

- 3 cups mixed salad greens
- 2 medium tomatoes, cut into wedges
- 2 hard-cooked eggs, cut into wedges
- 2 ounces Swiss cheese, cut into strips
- 2 carrots, sliced
- 1 cup diced, cooked beets
- 1 7-ounce can water-packed tuna, drained and flaked
- ¼ cup lite Italian dressing

Combine all ingredients, except dressing, in a large salad bowl; chill. Just before serving, toss with Italian dressing.

Slimmer's Danish Salad

Makes 6 servings.
Approximately 114 calories per serving.

- ¼ cup cold water
- ⅓ cup instant nonfat dry milk
- 1½ cups low-fat, small curd cottage cheese
- ⅓ cup crumbled Danish blue cheese
- 3 tablespoons lemon juice
- ¾ teaspoon onion salt
- ¼ teaspoon garlic salt
- 6 thick slices tomato
- 1 head iceberg lettuce, cleaned and chilled

Combine all ingredients, except tomato and lettuce, in a blender jar. Blend until smooth. Cover and chill. Cut lettuce into 6 narrow wedges. Arrange lettuce and tomato slices on salad plates. Spoon on dressing.

Rock Lobster Vegetable Salad

Makes 4 servings.
Approximately 153 calories per serving.

- 12 ounces cooked, rock lobster meat
- 1 cup plain low-fat yogurt
- 2 tablespoons Dijon-style mustard
  Juice of ½ lemon
  Lettuce leaves
- 1 10-ounce package frozen asparagus, cooked, drained, and chilled
- 1 cup chopped celery
- ¼ cup chopped red onion
  Capers

Slice lobster into medallions. Combine yogurt, mustard, and lemon juice; mix well. Add lobster; mix well. Place lettuce leaves on individual serving plates. Arrange vegetables on lettuce. Spoon lobster mixture on top. Garnish with capers.

Fruited Chicken Salad

Makes 8 servings.
Approximately 162 calories per serving without dressing.

- 1 fresh pineapple
- 3 cups cooked chicken, cut into large pieces
- 1 pint strawberries, washed, hulled and sliced
- 1 cup sliced celery
- ½ cup chopped walnuts
  Creamy Orange Dressing (Recipe on page 17.)

Cut pineapple in half lengthwise through the crown. Remove pulp, leaving shells intact. Core and dice pulp. Combine pineapple, chicken, strawberries, celery, and walnuts; toss lightly. Serve over crisp salad greens with Creamy Orange Dressing.

Strawberry-Pear Delight

Makes 6 servings.
Approximately 137 calories per serving.

- 2 3-ounce packages low-calorie strawberry gelatin
- 2 cups boiling water
- 1 cup low-calorie ginger ale or strawberry or cherry soda
- 4 ounce Neufchatel cheese, softened
- 2 tablespoons Lively Lemon French Dressing (Recipe on page 17)
- 2 fresh Bartlett pears
  Lemon juice
- ½ cup halved strawberries

Dissolve gelatin in boiling water. Stir in ginger ale. Pour into an 8-inch round layer pan; chill until firm. Combine cheese with dressing and beat until smooth. Halve and core pears. Chop 1 of the pears; fold into cheese mixture. Cut remaining pear into lengthwise slices; coat with lemon juice. Spread half of the pear-cheese mixture in an 8-inch circle in the center of a serving plate. Unmold gelatin "cake" on top of cheese mixture. Spread remaining pear-cheese mixture on top. Garnish with sliced pear and strawberries. Serve immediately.

Julienne Beef Garden Salad

Makes 6 servings.
Approximately 128 calories per serving.

- ½ head iceberg lettuce, torn into bite-size pieces
- 1 pound cooked lean beef, cut into julienne strips
- ¼ pound fresh mushrooms, sliced
- 1 cup thinly sliced celery
- ½ cucumber, sliced
- ⅓ cup halved, pitted ripe olives
- ⅓ cup sliced green onion
- 12 cherry tomatoes, halved
  Salt, optional

Combine lettuce, beef, mushrooms, celery, cucumber, olives, and onion; toss lightly. Cover and refrigerate until ready to serve. Add cherry tomatoes; toss gently. Serve with a favorite dressing.

Tomatoes Vinaigrette

Makes 6 servings.
Approximately 70 calories per serving.

- 4 large tomatoes, peeled and sliced
- 6 tablespoons chopped parsley
- 1 clove garlic, crushed
- 2 tablespoons vegetable oil
- 2 tablespoons cider vinegar
- 1 teaspoon salt
- 2 teaspoons minced dill
  Dash black pepper

Place tomatoes in a bowl. Sprinkle with parsley. Combine the garlic, oil, vinegar, salt, dill, and pepper; mix well. Pour over tomatoes and parsley. Cover. Chill at least 3 hours before serving.

Wash salad greens as soon as possible after purchasing them. Shake off the excess moisture and wrap the greens loosely in paper towels. Store in a plastic bag or in the hydrator of the refrigerator.

Fruit Salad

Makes 10 servings.
Approximately 102 calories per serving.

- ½ head lettuce
- 1 large, chilled honeydew melon
- 1 mango, seeded and chopped
- 4 bananas
- ¼ cup lemon juice
- 1 quart strawberries, washed and hulled
- 3 large oranges, chilled

Wash and drain lettuce; tear into bite-size pieces. Arrange lettuce on a serving tray or on 10 salad plates. Peel honeydew; seed and cut into thin slices. Arrange on tray. Sprinkle chopped mango over honeydew. Slice bananas; sprinkle on lemon juice. Arrange on tray. Scatter strawberries over top. Slice oranges. Edge salad with orange slices. Serve with Lime Dressing.

Lime Dressing

Approximately 30 calories per tablespoon.

- 1 cup prepared nondairy whipped topping
- 1 cup reduced calorie mayonnaise
- ⅓ cup lime juice
- ⅓ cup honey

Combine all ingredients and blend thoroughly.

Substitute plain, low-fat yogurt for mayonnaise in tuna, salmon, crab meat, ham, and chicken salads. Remember, one cup plain yogurt contains 150 calories; whereas one cup of mayonnaise sports a hefty 1,620 calories.

Plum Summery Salad

Makes 4 servings.
Approximately 142 calories per serving.

- 4 fresh plums, sliced
- 1 cup seedless grapes
- 1 cup sliced strawberries
- 1 cup cubed cantaloupe
  Juice of 1 lemon
- ½ cup fresh orange juice
- ¼ cup white wine
- ¼ teaspoon crushed tarragon
- 1 banana, peeled and sliced

Combine first 4 ingredients in a bowl; toss lightly with lemon juice. Combine orange juice, wine, and tarragon; pour over fruit. Marinate for 2 to 3 hours. Add banana before serving. Serve over cottage cheese, yogurt or with cold cuts.

Tangy Dressing

Makes 1 cup.
Approximately 9 calories per tablespoon.

- ½ cup low-fat creamed cottage cheese
- ½ cup tomato juice
- 1½ tablespoons tarragon wine vinegar
- ½ teaspoon prepared mustard
- ½ teaspoon Worcestershire sauce
- ¼ teaspoon garlic salt
- ¼ teaspoon celery salt

Combine all ingredients in a mixing bowl. Beat with rotary beater or blend in a blender.

Dessert Salad Dressing

Makes 1 cup.
Approximately 15 calories per tablespoon.

- ¼ cup plain low-fat yogurt
- 1 medium orange, sectioned
- ½ cup sliced banana
- 1 tablespoon honey
- 1 tablespoon lemon juice
- 1 teaspoon grated orange peel
- ¼ teaspoon salt

Place all ingredients in a blender container. Cover and blend until smooth.

Creamy Low-Calorie Dressing

Makes ¾ cup.
Approximately 16 calories per tablespoon.

- ½ cup buttermilk
- 2 tablespoons prepared mustard
- 1 tablespoon vinegar
- 1 tablespoon vegetable oil
- ¼ teaspoon salt

Combine all ingredients; stir until well blended. Serve as dressing with lettuce.

Dilly Dressing

Makes 1 cup.
Approximately 4 calories per tablespoon.

- 1 cup tomato juice
- 1 teaspoon grated lemon peel
- 2 tablespoons fresh lemon juice or wine vinegar
- 1 teaspoon salt
- ½ teaspoon fresh or dried dillweed
- ½ teaspoon dry mustard
- ¼ teaspoon liquid sugar substitute

Combine all ingredients in a jar; shake to blend. Chill. Serve over a tossed salad or sliced tomatoes and onion rings.

Lively Lemon French Dressing

Makes 1 cup.
Approximately 10 calories per tablespoon.

    1 teaspoon unflavored gelatin
    1 tablespoon cold water
    ¼ cup boiling water
    2 tablespoons sugar
    ½ teaspoon salt
    1 teaspoon grated lemon peel
    ½ cup fresh lemon juice
    ¼ teaspoon garlic salt
      Dash black pepper
    ⅛ teaspoon dry mustard
    ¼ teaspoon Worcestershire sauce

Soften gelatin in cold water. Add boiling water; stir until dissolved. Add sugar and salt and stir until dissolved. Combine gelatin mixture with remaining ingredients in a container with a tight fitting lid; shake well. May be covered and stored in refrigerator until needed. If refrigerated before serving, place container in a pan of hot water for 5 minutes to liquefy the gelatin. Serve cool, but not chilled, over crisp salad greens.

Low-Calorie Thousand Island Dressing

Makes 1½ cups.
Approximately 14 calories per tablespoon.

    1 8-ounce carton plain low-fat yogurt
    ¼ cup catsup
    1 teaspoon prepared mustard
    ½ teaspoon prepared horseradish
    ½ teaspoon onion salt
      Dash black pepper
    1 hard-cooked egg, diced
    3 tablespoons chopped dill pickle

Combine yogurt, catsup, mustard, horseradish, salt, and pepper; mix well. Stir in egg and pickle.

Creamy Orange Dressing

Makes ⅔ cup.
Approximately 34 calories per tablespoon.

    ⅓ cup imitation sour cream
    ¼ cup honey
    1 tablespoon grated orange peel
    1 tablespoon fresh orange juice
    ¼ teaspoon salt
    ½ teaspoon mint flakes

Combine all ingredients in a blender jar; blend until smooth.

Rosy Italian Dressing

Makes 1¼ cups.
Approximately 11 calories per tablespoon.

    1 cup tomato juice
    1 teaspoon cornstarch
    2 teaspoons onion salt
    ¼ cup vinegar
    1 tablespoon vegetable oil
    ¼ teaspoon mixed Italian herbs

Combine tomato juice, cornstarch, and onion salt in a small saucepan. Cook over moderate heat, stirring, until mixture boils and is slightly thickened. Remove from heat and cool. Pour into a small jar. Add remaining ingredients; cover and shake well. Shake again just before using.

Lite Horseradish Dressing

Makes 1¾ cups.
Approximately 8 calories per tablespoon.

    16 ounces creamed low-fat cottage cheese
    1 tablespoon skim milk
    1 tablespoon lemon juice
    ½ teaspoon salt
    ½ teaspoon horseradish
    2 strips pimiento
    1 medium carrot, cut into pieces
    3 sprigs parsley

Blend first 5 ingredients at high speed until smooth. Add pimiento, carrots, and parsley. Turn blender on and off quickly to barely chop vegetables. Chill before serving.

Blue Cheese Dressing

Makes 1⅓ cups.
Approximately 15 calories per tablespoon.

    1 cup low-fat cottage cheese
    2½ tablespoons lemon juice
    ⅓ cup nonfat dry milk
    1 teaspoon seasoned salt
    ¼ teaspoon prepared horseradish
      Pinch white pepper
    2 tablespoons crumbled blue cheese

Combine cottage cheese, lemon juice, milk, salt, horseradish, and pepper in blender jar; blend until smooth. Stir blue cheese into the cottage cheese mixture.

Vegetables

Nectarines and Tomatoes

Makes 4 servings.
Approximately 59 calories per serving.

- 4 large nectarines
- 2 cups plum tomatoes
- 1 tablespoon margarine
  Salt and pepper
- 1 tablespoon minced mint or green onion

Halve, pit, and cut nectarines into generous slices. Halve tomatoes or leave whole, if preferred. Melt margarine in a skillet. Add nectarines and sauté over moderate heat 1 minute. Add tomatoes and continue cooking until hot and glazed, about 1 to 2 minutes longer. Do not overcook. Shake pan or stir gently during cooking. Season lightly with salt and pepper to taste and sprinkle with mint or green onion.

Broccoli with Sunshine Sauce

Makes 3 servings.
Approximately 40 calories per serving.

- 1 10-ounce package frozen broccoli spears
- 1 chicken bouillon cube
- 2 teaspoons prepared mustard
- 1 tablespoon nonfat dry milk

Cook broccoli in ½ cup water seasoned with bouillon cube, until just tender-crisp. Remove broccoli to a serving dish; stir mustard and dry milk into hot liquid. Pour sauce over broccoli.

Stir-Fried Asparagus a la Lemon

Makes 4 servings.
Approximately 86 calories per serving.

- 1½ pounds fresh asparagus, sliced
- 1 small onion, sliced
- 1 small clove garlic, minced
- 1 chicken bouillon cube
- 1 tablespoon margarine
- 2 tablespoons sliced almonds
  Grated peel and juice of ½ lemon

Place asparagus, onion, garlic, bouillon cube, and margarine in a frying pan. Stir-fry until asparagus is just tender, 5 to 7 minutes. Stir in almonds, lemon peel and juice; heat through.

Zucchini Gondolas

Makes 6 servings.
Approximately 175 calories per serving.

- 3 medium-size zucchini
- ½ cup ricotta cheese or cottage cheese
- ¼ cup diced ham
- ½ green pepper, chopped
- 1 egg, lightly beaten
- 1 1½-ounce package spaghetti sauce mix
- 1 tablespoon grated Parmesan cheese
- 1 cup tomato juice

Preheat oven to 350°. Cut each zucchini in half lengthwise; scoop out centers, leaving ¼-inch shells. Simmer shells in 1 inch water in a covered pan for 6 to 8 minutes, until tender-crisp. Chop zucchini pulp. Combine zucchini with cheese, ham, green pepper, egg, and 2 teaspoons of the spaghetti sauce mix. Arrange zucchini shells in a single layer in a shallow baking dish; fill with cheese mixture. Sprinkle Parmesan cheese on top. Combine remaining spaghetti sauce mix with tomato juice; pour into pan around zucchini. Bake for 20 to 25 minutes, until filling is firm and zucchini tender.

Bring zest to a low-calorie meal by adding a clove or two of garlic. No need to worry about calories. Each clove of garlic contains only one to two calories and will add a gourmet touch to your slender fixin's.

Carrot-Celery Medley

Makes 4 servings.
Approximately 46 calories per serving.

- 1 tablespoon margarine
- 1 cup thinly sliced carrots
- 1 cup diagonally sliced celery
- ½ cup thin strips green pepper
  Salt and pepper to taste
  Dillweed

Melt margarine in a heavy frying pan; add carrots, celery, and green pepper. Cover and simmer over moderate heat about 7 minutes. Season to taste with salt and pepper. Add a dash of dillweed. Cook over low heat until vegetables are just tender, about 5 minutes.

Broccoli with Sunshine Sauce
Carrot-Celery Medley
Nectarines and Tomatoes

Deviled Tomatoes

Makes 8 servings.
Approximately 40 calories per serving.

- 4 large tomatoes, halved
  Salt
- 1 tablespoon prepared mustard
- 2 tablespoons chopped green pepper
- 2 tablespoons diced celery
- 1 tablespoon chopped green onion
- 1 tablespoon chopped parsley
- 1 tablespoon margarine, melted

Place tomatoes, cut side up, in a 9 x 13-inch baking dish. Sprinkle on salt to taste. Spread cut side of tomatoes with the prepared mustard. Mix the remaining ingredients together and spoon the mixture over the top of the mustard. Bake in a 425° oven for 8 to 10 minutes.

Evergreen Zucchini

Makes 8 servings.
Approximately 50 calories per serving.

- 1 tablespoon salt
- 1½ cups water
- 8 to 10 medium zucchini squash (about 3 pounds), cut into ½-inch slices
- 1 cup chopped parsley
- 1 tablespoon margarine, softened
- 2 tablespoons instant minced onion
- ½ teaspoon grated lemon peel
- 2 tablespoons fresh lemon juice

Place salt and water in a frying pan. Add zucchini; cover and cook until just tender, 8 to 10 minutes; drain. Add remaining ingredients; heat, stirring occasionally.

Lemon Cabbage

Makes 6 servings.
Approximately 57 calories per serving.

- 2 tablespoons margarine
- ½ teaspoon caraway seed
- 1 medium head cabbage (about 1½ pounds), coarsely chopped
  Grated peel and juice of ½ lemon
  Dash black pepper

Place margarine and caraway seed in a large frying pan. Heat until margarine is melted. Add cabbage. Cook over high heat for 3 to 4 minutes, stirring constantly. Reduce heat and cover. Simmer for 2 to 3 minutes, until just tender. Stir in lemon peel and juice. Season with pepper.

Baked Fries

Makes 6 servings.
Approximately 50 calories per serving.

- 3 medium potatoes, peeled
- 1 egg white, lightly beaten
  Seasoned salt, Parmesan cheese or packaged salad dressing mix
  Crushed cornflakes, bread crumbs or sesame seed

Preheat oven to 425°. Cut potatoes lengthwise into eighths. Brush wedges with egg white. Sprinkle on seasonings and bread crumbs. Bake on a baking sheet 30 to 35 minutes.

Beet-Onion Supreme

Makes 4 servings.
Approximately 70 calories per serving.

- 1 tablespoon margarine
- 1 16-ounce can sliced beets, drained, reserve 2 tablespoons liquid
- 1 cup thinly sliced onion
- ¼ cup chopped celery
  Salt and pepper
- 1 tablespoon chopped parsley

Melt margarine in a medium skillet or saucepan. Add beets, reserved liquid, onion, and celery. Cover and cook over low heat until onion and celery are tender, about 10 to 12 minutes. Season with salt and pepper to taste. Sprinkle chopped parsley over top.

Braised Cucumbers

Makes 2 servings cucumbers, 2 servings broth.
Approximately 51 calories per serving.

- 2 large cucumbers (approximately 1 pound), peeled
- 1 can chicken broth
- ½ cup diagonally sliced celery
- 1 tablespoon diced pimiento
- ½ teaspoon lemon juice
  Generous dash dried chervil leaves, crushed

Slice cucumbers in half lengthwise; remove seeds. Cut into 1-inch pieces. Combine all ingredients in a saucepan; cover and bring to a boil. Simmer for 5 minutes, stirring occasionally; do not drain. Chill. Drain, reserving broth. Add enough water to reserved broth to make 10 ounces. Heat broth mixture in saucepan, stirring occasionally. Serve in cups.

Corn Delight

Makes 6 servings.
Approximately 43 calories per serving.

- 1 10-ounce package frozen whole kernel corn
- ½ cup diced celery
- 1 chicken bouillon cube, crushed
- ⅓ cup water
- 1 4-ounce can sliced mushrooms, drained
- 1 medium tomato, cut into thin wedges
  Salt and pepper

In a medium saucepan, combine corn, celery, bouillon cube, and water. Bring to a boil; cover and simmer until vegetables are tender, about 5 to 7 minutes. Stir in mushrooms and tomato wedges; heat through. Season with salt and pepper to taste.

German-Style Green Beans

Makes 4 servings.
Approximately 85 calories per serving.

- 1 16-ounce can green beans, drained, reserve 2 tablespoons liquid
- 2 tablespoons vinegar
- ¼ pound bacon, sliced
- ⅓ cup chopped onion
- 1 tablespoon flour
- ½ teaspoon sugar
- ½ teaspoon salt
  Dash black pepper

Combine bean liquid with vinegar; set aside. In a large frying pan, fry bacon until crisp; remove and drain on paper toweling. Remove all but 3 tablespoons of fat from the frying pan. Add onion and cook until soft, but not brown. Blend in flour, sugar, salt, and pepper. Add reserved liquid all at once. Cook quickly, stirring constantly until mixture thickens. Add beans and heat thoroughly. Crumble bacon over beans before serving.

Peas a la Sesame

Makes 2 servings.
Approximately 88 calories per serving.

- 1 8½-ounce can peas, undrained
- 1 teaspoon margarine
- 3 tablespoons slivered celery
- ¼ teaspoon sesame seed
  Salt

Heat peas in liquid. Melt margarine in a small frying pan. Add celery and sesame seed and sauté until celery is just tender. Drain peas; toss lightly with celery mixture and salt to taste.

Creamed Green Beans and Mushrooms

Makes 4 servings.
Approximately 75 calories per serving.

- 1 cup Skinny White Sauce
- 1½ cups cut green beans, cooked
- 1 cup mushroom slices, cooked
- ¼ teaspoon crushed basil

Combine white sauce, green beans, mushrooms, and basil leaves in a medium-size saucepan. Cook over moderate heat, stirring occasionally, about 3 minutes or until thoroughly heated.

Skinny White Sauce

Makes 1 cup.
Approximately 218 calories per cup.

- 1 tablespoon cornstarch
- ¼ teaspoon salt
  Dash black pepper
- 1 cup skim milk
- 1 tablespoon margarine

Combine cornstarch, salt, and pepper in a 2-quart saucepan. Gradually stir in milk until smooth. Add margarine. Bring to a boil over medium heat, stirring constantly. Boil for 1 minute, stirring constantly.

Baked Cabbage Wedges

Makes 6 servings.
Approximately 138 calories per serving.

- 1 medium head cabbage
- 1 green pepper, julienned
- 1 cup boiling chicken broth
- ¼ cup flour
- 1 teaspoon salt
  Dash black pepper
- 8 ounces low-fat cottage cheese, sieved
- ½ cup sour half and half
- 2 tablespoons tomato paste
- ½ cup sliced dill pickles

Preheat oven to 350°. Rinse cabbage. Cut into 1-inch wedges; remove core. Simmer cabbage and green pepper in chicken broth for 7 minutes or until just tender. Arrange vegetables in a buttered 8-inch baking dish. Stir flour into broth. Add seasonings. Cook until thickened, stirring constantly. Blend in cottage cheese, sour half and half, and tomato paste. Add dill pickles. Pour sauce over vegetables. Bake for 30 minutes.

Beef

Celery Beef Bake

Makes 8 servings.
Approximately 230 calories per serving.

Water
2½ teaspoons salt, divided
  1 stalk celery, cut in ¼-inch slices (about 5 cups)
  1 15-ounce carton low-fat cottage cheese
  4 medium eggs
2½ teaspoons Italian seasoning, divided
1½ teaspoons onion powder, divided
  1 pound lean ground beef
     Dash black pepper
  1 1-pound can whole tomatoes, drained, broken up
  2 ounces part skim mozzarella cheese, thinly sliced

Preheat oven to 325°. In a medium saucepan, bring 1 inch water and ½ teaspoon of the salt to a boil. Add celery; cover and cook until almost tender, about 8 minutes; drain. In a small bowl, mix cottage cheese, 3 of the eggs, 1½ teaspoons of the Italian seasoning, 1 teaspoon of the salt, and ½ teaspoon of the onion powder. In a medium frying pan, brown beef, stirring frequently; drain fat. Stir in remaining 1 teaspoon each salt, Italian seasoning, and onion powder. Add pepper, tomatoes, and remaining egg; mix well. Spoon half of the celery into a 2-quart casserole. Spread half of the cottage cheese mixture on top; cover with half of the ground beef; repeat. Bake, uncovered, for 25 minutes. Top with mozzarella; bake until cheese is melted, about 10 minutes.

Brazilian Rump Roast with Fruit Garnish

Makes 8 servings.
About 340 calories per serving.

  1 tablespoon shortening
  4 pounds rolled beef rump roast
  1 cup chopped onion
  1 clove garlic, minced
  2 teaspoons instant coffee
  1 teaspoon salt
  1 cup tomato juice
  1 tablespoon lemon juice
  1 cup water
  1 tablespoon cornstarch
     Sliced orange cartwheels, optional

Heat shortening in a Dutch oven. Brown meat on all sides. Combine onion, garlic, instant coffee,

salt, ¼ cup of the tomato juice, and lemon juice. Pour over meat. Cover and cook slowly until meat is tender, 2½ to 3 hours, turning occasionally. More tomato juice may be added, if needed. Remove roast to a serving platter. Remove excess fat from pan drippings. Combine remaining tomato juice, water, and cornstarch; mix well. Stir into drippings; cook until thickened, stirring constantly. Serve with sliced meat. Garnish roast with orange cartwheels.

Reduce smoke and odor when broiling by placing a few slices of stale bread under the broiler pan or rack. The bread absorbs the grease in the pan and helps prevent smoke.

Beef Stroganoff

Makes 4 servings.
Approximately 230 calories per serving. Noodles extra calories.

  1 pound flank steak
  1 cup beef broth
  1 cup chopped onion
  1 pound fresh mushrooms, cleaned and sliced
¼ cup cold water
  1 tablespoon flour
  1 tablespoon cornstarch
¼ cup low-fat plain yogurt, at room temperature
½ teaspoon paprika
¾ teaspoon salt
¼ teaspoon garlic powder
½ teaspoon prepared mustard

Preheat broiler. Broil steak 6 inches from heat until rare, about 5 minutes on each side. Cut diagonally into thin, 2-inch strips; set aside. In a large frying pan, bring broth to a boil. Add onion and mushrooms. Simmer, covered, about 5 minutes until vegetables are tender. Remove vegetables with a slotted spoon; set aside. Simmer broth until reduced to ½ cup; remove from heat. Combine water, flour, and cornstarch; mix well. Stir into broth with a wire whisk. Cook and stir over low heat until thickened, about 2 minutes. Remove from heat. Combine yogurt, paprika, salt, garlic powder, and mustard. Add to thickened broth, stirring until smooth. Mix in reserved beef, onion and mushrooms. Warm over very low heat, stirring constantly, until hot, about 5 minutes. Serve over noodles, if desired.

Sauerbraten

Makes 10 servings.
Approximately 350 calories per serving.

    3 pounds boneless beef rump roast
1½ cups cider vinegar
    1 cup beef broth
    2 tablespoons instant minced onion
    2 teaspoons salt
    6 whole cloves
    6 whole black peppercorns
    2 bay leaves

Trim fat from meat. Place meat in a covered glass or enamel bowl. Combine remaining ingredients; pour over beef. Cover and refrigerate for 3 to 4 days, turning occasionally. Place meat and the marinade in a large saucepan. Bring to the boiling point. Reduce heat, cover, and simmer until tender, 2½ to 3 hours. If necessary, add water to liquid in saucepan during cooking. Refrigerate until fat is firm; remove fat and whole spices. Reheat the meat and liquid. Place meat on a heated platter; slice. Pour liquid over meat.

Herbed Beef and Vegetable Kebabs

Makes 8 servings.
Approximately 300 calories per serving.

    2 pounds boneless beef round or sirloin steak,
      cut into 1-inch cubes
¼ cup vegetable oil
    2 tablespoons wine vinegar
    1 tablespoon onion powder
    1 tablespoon crushed basil
    1 teaspoon garlic powder
    1 teaspoon salt
¼ teaspoon crushed thyme
¼ teaspoon black pepper
    1 pound zucchini, cut into ½-inch chunks
    8 medium, fresh mushrooms
    8 cherry tomatoes

Place beef in a covered bowl. Combine oil, vinegar, onion powder, basil, garlic powder, salt, thyme, and pepper; mix well. Pour over beef; toss to coat. Cover and refrigerate for 2 hours. Alternately thread meat and zucchini on skewers; place a mushroom on the end of each skewer. Brush vegetables with marinade. Arrange on a rack in a broiler pan. Place under a preheated broiler and cook as desired, turning and brushing with marinade occasionally. Place 1 tomato at the end of each skewer and broil 1 minute.

Steak-Vegetable Duo

Makes 4 servings.
Approximately 387 calories per serving.

1½ pounds boneless round steak, cut ¾ inch thick
1½ teaspoons salt
¼ teaspoon dry mustard
    Dash black pepper
¼ cup chopped onion
    2 cloves garlic, crushed
¼ cup water
    1 8¼-ounce can whole peeled tomatoes,
      drained, reserve juice
    1 tablespoon cornstarch
    3 cups sliced zucchini
    1 10-ounce package frozen leaf spinach,
      thawed and cut into pieces

Trim fat from steak and cut into 4 pieces. Slowly heat trimmed fat in a large frying pan to obtain 1 tablespoon drippings. Discard unneeded fat. Brown steak on both sides. Combine salt, dry mustard, and pepper; sprinkle over meat. Add onion, garlic, and water; cover tightly and cook slowly 75 minutes, or until meat is tender. Remove meat from pan. Blend reserved tomato juice with cornstarch; combine with cooking liquid and cook, stirring constantly, until thickened. Stir in tomatoes, zucchini, and spinach. Place meat on top of vegetables and cook slowly, covered, 8 to 10 minutes. Remove meat to warm platter. Place vegetables and sauce on platter with meat.

Marinated Flank Steak

Makes 6 servings.
Approximately 208 calories per serving.

    1 10¾-ounce can tomato soup
⅓ cup Burgundy wine
    2 tablespoons finely chopped ripe olives
    1 small clove garlic, minced
    1 tablespoon minced onion
1½ pounds flank steak, scored

Combine all ingredients, except steak, in a shallow baking dish. Add steak and marinate at room temperature for 1 hour, turning once. Remove steak. Pour marinade into a saucepan. Cover and simmer for 10 minutes. Stir occasionally. Broil steak 4 inches from heat about 4 minutes on each side or until desired doneness, brushing with sauce. Reheat remaining sauce; serve with steak.

Swedish Cabbage Casserole

Makes 6 servings.
Approximately 241 calories per serving.

    1   tablespoon vegetable oil
    1   pound lean ground beef
    ½   cup chopped onion
    1   16-ounce can stewed tomatoes
    ½   cup instant rice
    1   8-ounce can tomato sauce
    ½   cup cubed pasteurized process American cheese
    1   tablespoon Worcestershire sauce
    ½   teaspoon salt
    ¼   teaspoon garlic salt
    3   cups shredded cabbage

Heat oil in a large frying pan. Brown ground beef and onion until onion is tender; drain fat. Add tomatoes and rice, stirring to break tomatoes; blend thoroughly. Bring to a boil, cover and turn off heat. Let stand for 10 minutes. Stir in next 5 ingredients and heat until cheese is melted. Arrange cabbage in the bottom of an 11 x 7 x 2-inch pan. Spread hamburger mixture over cabbage. Cover and bake at 350° for 30 minutes.

Liver Strips in Vegetable Puree

Makes 4 servings.
Approximately 202 calories per serving. Rice extra calories.

    2   beef bouillon cubes, crushed
    1   cup hot water
    2   medium carrots, sliced crosswise
    1   cup sliced onion
    ¾   cup sliced celery
    1   bay leaf
    1   pound beef liver, cut into ½-inch slices
    ¼   teaspoon salt
        Dash pepper
    ¼   cup rosé wine
    2   tablespoons diced pimiento
        Cooked rice, optional

Place bouillon cubes and water in a large frying pan. Heat until bouillon dissolves. Add carrots, onion, and celery; cover and cook for 15 minutes. Add bay leaf. Place liver on top of vegetables; sprinkle on salt and pepper; add wine. Cover and cook slowly for 20 minutes or until liver is tender, turning occasionally. Remove liver and set aside. Discard bay leaf. Blend vegetables and liquid in an electric blender until smooth; return to frying pan. Cut liver in 2 x ½-inch strips. Add liver and pimiento to vegetable puree; heat through. Serve over cooked rice.

Braised Beef Slimmer

Makes 4 servings.
Approximately 315 calories per serving.

    1   tablespoon vegetable oil
    1½   pounds beef round steak, ¾ to 1 inch thick, fat trimmed, and cut into 1-inch cubes
    1   teaspoon salt
    ½   teaspoon thyme
          Dash black pepper
    1   beef bouillon cube
    ½   cup hot water
    2   10-ounce packages cut Italian green beans, thawed
    8   ounces mushrooms, cleaned and sliced
    ¾   cup buttermilk
    1   tablespoon cornstarch

Heat oil in a frying pan or Dutch oven. Add beef and brown on all sides. Combine salt, thyme, and pepper; sprinkle over meat. Crush bouillon cube and dissolve in hot water; add to meat. Cover tightly and cook slowly 1½ hours. Stir in green beans and mushrooms. Cook, covered, for about 13 minutes. Add buttermilk to cornstarch, stirring to blend. Gradually add buttermilk to meat mixture and cook until thickened, stirring occasionally.

Broiled Liver Kebabs

Makes 6 servings.
Approximately 235 calories per serving.

    1   cup tomato juice
    2½   tablespoons instant minced onion
    1   tablespoon lemon juice
    1   teaspoon Italian seasoning
    1   teaspoon salt
    ¼   teaspoon garlic powder
          Dash black pepper
    2   pounds beef liver, cut 1 inch thick
    2   medium zucchini, sliced ¾ inch thick
    6 to 12   medium whole mushrooms
    6   cherry tomatoes

Combine tomato juice, onion, lemon juice, Italian seasoning, salt, garlic powder, and pepper; mix well. Cut liver into 1-inch pieces; place in a bowl. Pour tomato marinade over liver. Cover and refrigerate at least 5 hours or overnight, turning at least once. Remove liver from marinade; drain. Using 6 skewers, alternately thread liver, zucchini, and mushrooms on skewers. Baste with marinade. Place under preheated broiler. Broil 8 to 10 minutes or until desired doneness, basting occasionally. Cap each skewer with a cherry tomato and broil 1 minute.

Pepper Steak

Makes 6 servings.
Approximately 208 calories per serving. Rice extra calories.

- 1 tablespoon margarine
- 1½ pounds round steak, thinly sliced
- ⅓ cup chopped onion
- 1 1-pound can stewed tomatoes
- ¼ cup water
- 2 teaspoons instant beef bouillon
- ⅛ teaspoon garlic powder
- 2 tablespoons soy sauce
- 2 tablespoons cornstarch
- 1 green pepper, thinly sliced
  Cooked rice, optional

Melt margarine in a frying pan. Brown steak and onion. Add tomatoes, water, bouillon, and garlic powder. Cover and simmer for 1 hour or until beef is tender. Blend soy sauce and cornstarch; add to beef mixture; stir constantly until mixture thickens. Add green pepper and simmer 10 minutes, stirring occasionally. Serve over rice.

Parsleyed Oven Pot Roast

Makes 10 servings.
Approximately 375 calories per serving.

- 2½ teaspoons salt, divided
- ¼ teaspoon black pepper
- 4½ to 5 pounds lean bottom round of beef
- 1 28-ounce can tomatoes, broken up
- ¾ cup dry red wine
- ¼ cup instant minced onion
- 2 tablespoons parsley flakes
- 1 bay leaf
- ½ teaspoon instant minced garlic
- 6 medium carrots, peeled and sliced
- 1½ pounds zucchini, sliced
- 2 cups cherry tomatoes, pricked with fork

Preheat oven to 450°. Rub 1½ teaspoons of the salt and the pepper over surface of meat. Place meat, fat side down, in a heavy, ovenproof casserole or Dutch oven. Brown on both sides in oven about 50 to 60 minutes. Drain fat. Combine tomatoes, wine, onion, parsley, bay leaf, garlic, and remaining 1 teaspoon salt. Pour over meat. Cover and reduce heat to 350°. Bake 2½ to 3 hours or until meat and vegetables are tender. Add the carrots 40 minutes before cooking time is up; the zucchini 20 minutes before; the cherry tomatoes 10 minutes before. Slice steak and serve with the vegetables.

Hawaiian Meatballs

Makes 4 servings.
Approximately 283 calories per serving.

- 1½ pounds lean ground beef
- 2 tablespoons minced green onion
- 2 tablespoons minced green pepper
- ½ teaspoon salt
- 1 tablespoon vegetable oil
- 1 10¾-ounce can tomato soup
- ⅓ cup water
- ½ cup crushed pineapple in unsweetened juice, drained
- 1 teaspoon soy sauce
  Dash ground ginger
  Cooked noodles or rice, optional

Combine beef, onion, green pepper, and salt; mix well. Shape into 24 meatballs. Heat oil in a large frying pan. Brown meatballs over medium heat; drain fat. Add soup, water, pineapple, soy sauce, and ginger. Cover and cook over low heat for 20 minutes, stirring occasionally.

Sunny Flank Steak

Makes 4 servings.
Approximately 311 calories per serving.

- 3 medium oranges
- ⅓ cup lemon juice
- 3 tablespoons Worcestershire sauce
- 2 tablespoons vegetable oil
- 2 teaspoons sugar
- 1 teaspoon salt
- ⅛ teaspoon ground cloves
- 4 drops Tabasco sauce
- 1¼ pounds beef flank steak

Grate peel from 1 of the oranges to measure 1 teaspoon; cut orange in half and squeeze juice into a small saucepan. Add lemon juice, Worcestershire sauce, oil, sugar, salt, cloves, and Tabasco; heat to boiling, stirring to dissolve sugar; cool. Place steak in a plastic bag and add marinade, turning to coat. Tie bag securely, pressing out air. Place in a utility dish. Marinate in refrigerator 6 hours or overnight, turning at least once. Remove steak from marinade and place in broiler pan. Broil 3 to 4 inches from heat for 5 to 6 minutes. Brush steak with marinade. Turn and broil second side of steak 5 to 6 minutes (rare). Carve steak diagonally into very thin slices. Garnish with wedges cut from remaining 2 oranges.

Festive Filled Grilled Steaks

Makes 8 servings.
Approximately 363 calories per serving.

- ¾ cup lite Italian dressing
- ⅓ cup dry red wine
- 2 1½-pound lean chuck steaks, 1-inch thick and trimmed of fat
- 1 tablespoon margarine
- ½ pound fresh mushrooms, sliced
- ¼ cup chopped parsley
- 2 tablespoons chopped onion

In a large baking dish, blend Italian dressing and wine. Add steaks; marinate in refrigerator, turning occasionally, at least 4 hours. In a small skillet, melt margarine; sauté mushrooms until tender. Add parsley and onion. Place mushroom mixture on 1 steak and top with the other steak; tie securely with string. Grill or broil, turning frequently, until desired doneness.

Stuffed Peppers Trinidad

Makes 4 servings.
Approximately 225 calories per serving.

- 4 green peppers
- 2 teaspoons margarine
- 3 tablespoons minced onion
- ½ pound lean ground beef
- 1 cup cooked rice
- ½ teaspoon salt
- ⅛ teaspoon paprika
- 1 teaspoon bitters
- 1 16-ounce can tomatoes

Preheat oven to 375°. Cook peppers in boiling water until just tender; drain. Melt margarine in a large frying pan. Sauté onion and ground beef until onion is tender. Add rice, salt, paprika, and bitters. Cut tops off peppers; remove seeds. Fill peppers with meat and rice mixture; place in a casserole. Pour tomatoes around peppers. Bake for 25 minutes, until heated through.

Skewered Steak Strips

Makes 6 servings.
Approximately 252 calories per serving.

- 2 pounds top round steak, 1¼ to 1½ inches thick, cut into ¼-inch strips
- 1 cup low-calorie blue cheese dressing
- 2 tablespoons lemon juice
- 12 medium mushrooms
- 12 cherry tomatoes

Place steak in a plastic bag. Combine dressing and lemon juice; pour into bag, mixing to coat strips. Tie bag securely, pressing out air. Place in a utility dish and marinate in refrigerator 4 to 6 hours or overnight. Drain marinade from meat and reserve. Alternately thread beef strips, weaving back and forth, with mushrooms and tomatoes on four 12- to 15-inch skewers. Charcoal grill or broil 3 to 4 inches from heat. Broil 3 minutes, brushing occasionally with reserved marinade. Turn and broil to desired degree of doneness, 3 to 4 minutes, brushing with marinade.

Beef and Mushroom Kebabs

Makes 6 servings.
Approximately 319 calories per serving.

- 2 tablespoons vegetable oil
- ¼ cup Worcestershire sauce
- 2 tablespoons catsup
- 2 tablespoons lemon juice
- 1 tablespoon honey or light corn syrup
- 1 to 1½ pounds boneless chuck steak, fat trimmed, cut into 1-inch cubes
- 8 to 12 mushroom caps
- 2 green peppers, cut into squares

Combine oil, Worcestershire sauce, catsup, lemon juice, and honey; pour over steak and refrigerate 30 to 60 minutes. Alternately thread steak, mushrooms, and peppers on 4 to 6 skewers. Grill over hot coals or broil for 10 to 15 minutes, turning occasionally and brushing with marinade.

Steak and Vegetables Fuji

Makes 4 servings.
Approximately 250 calories per serving.

- 1 pound round steak
- 1¼ cups water
- 1 envelope mushroom gravy mix
- 2 to 3 tablespoons soy sauce
- 1 16-ounce can bean sprouts, drained
- 1 8-ounce can sliced water chestnuts, drained
- 1 10-ounce package fresh spinach leaves (about 6 cups), cleaned, stems removed

Cut steak into very thin slices. In a large frying pan, combine water, gravy mix, and soy sauce. Bring to a boil, stirring constantly. Add steak and simmer until meat is no longer red. Stir in bean sprouts and water chestnuts. Place spinach on top of meat mixture; cover with lid or foil. Simmer for 2 to 3 minutes or just until spinach wilts.

Brunch Beef Soufflé

Makes 8 servings.
Approximately 272 calories per serving.

1 pound lean ground beef
1½ teaspoons salt
¼ teaspoon nutmeg
Dash black pepper
6 eggs
1½ cups skim milk
5 slices white bread, cubed
4 ounces Swiss cheese, shredded
1 tablespoon diced pimiento

Preheat oven to 325°. Brown ground beef in a large nonstick frying pan; drain fat. Sprinkle salt, nutmeg, and pepper over ground beef; let cool. Beat eggs well; stir in milk; fold in bread cubes, cheese, and pimiento. Stir in ground beef. Place mixture in a greased 8-inch casserole or utility dish; cover and refrigerate overnight. Bake for 1 hour 10 minutes. Let stand 5 minutes before cutting into serving-size pieces.

Texas Hash

Makes 6 servings.
Approximately 207 calories per serving.

1 pound lean ground beef
2 large onions, sliced
1 green pepper, cut into thin strips
2 teaspoons chili powder
2 teaspoons salt
Dash black pepper
1 1-pound can tomatoes
½ cup raw rice

Brown ground beef, onion, and green pepper in a large frying pan; drain fat. Sprinkle chili powder, salt, and pepper over meat. Add tomatoes and rice. Bring to a boil; reduce heat, cover, and cook until rice is tender, 25 to 30 minutes.

Cornburger Skillet

Makes 4 servings.
Approximately 360 calories per serving.

1 tablespoon vegetable oil
1 pound lean ground beef
⅔ cup chopped onion
1 teaspoon salt
⅛ teaspoon garlic salt
Dash black pepper
1 17-ounce can whole kernel corn, drained
¾ cup grated, pasteurized process American cheese

Heat oil in a large frying pan. Sauté beef and onion until onion is tender; drain fat. Stir in seasonings and corn. Heat through. Top with grated cheese; cover frying pan. Simmer for 5 minutes or until cheese melts.

Caribbean Lime Steak

Makes 6 servings.
Approximately 302 calories per serving.

⅓ cup fresh lime juice (about 3 medium limes)
2 tablespoons vegetable oil
¼ cup molasses
2 tablespoons prepared mustard
1 teaspoon grated lime peel
1 teaspoon garlic powder
½ teaspoon black pepper
½ teaspoon salt
2 pounds lean flank steak
Lime wedges

Combine all ingredients, except steak, in a small bowl; mix lightly with a wire whisk. Score steak across top. Pour lime juice mixture over steak; turn to coat all sides. Refrigerate 4 to 8 hours, turning once or twice. Preheat broiler. Broil steak 3 inches from heat for 3 minutes on each side (for medium-rare) or grill over charcoal. Thinly slice on the diagonal. Serve garnished with lime wedges.

Shanghai Meatballs

Makes 4 servings.
Approximately 287 calories per serving. Rice extra calories.

1 egg, lightly beaten
1 tablespoon minced green onion
1 teaspoon ground ginger
¾ teaspoon salt
⅛ teaspoon garlic powder
1 5-ounce can water chestnuts, drained and chopped
1 pound lean ground beef
1 tablespoon vegetable oil
1 ¾-ounce envelope brown gravy mix
1 cup water
½ cup diagonally sliced sweet pickle

Combine egg, onion, ginger, salt, garlic powder, and water chestnuts; mix lightly. Add ground beef; mix well. Shape into small meatballs. Heat oil in a large frying pan. Brown meatballs in oil over medium heat; drain fat. Add gravy mix and water; simmer until thickened, stirring constantly. Add pickle. Serve with rice.

Chicken Breasts a la Citron

Makes 4 servings.
Approximately 230 calories per serving.

- 2 oranges, peeled, sliced into thick cartwheels
- 2 tablespoons sauterne or other dry white wine
- 2 whole chicken breasts (about ¾ pound each), split, skinned
- ½ teaspoon curry powder
- ½ teaspoon grated orange peel
- ¼ cup fresh orange juice
- 1 tablespoon honey
- 2 teaspoons prepared mustard
- ½ teaspoon salt

Preheat oven to 350°. Sprinkle orange cartwheels with sauterne; marinate at room temperature while preparing chicken. Rub chicken on all sides with curry powder; arrange in an 8- or 9-inch square baking pan. Combine orange peel, juice, honey, mustard, and salt. Pour over chicken. Cover baking pan with foil. Bake for 30 minutes. Uncover and bake 15 minutes or until chicken is tender. Drain oranges, reserving marinade. Arrange chicken and oranges on a serving platter. Spoon off excess fat from pan drippings. Stir in reserved marinade. Serve sauce with chicken.

Chicken Broccoli Casserole

Makes 6 servings.
Approximately 223 calories per serving.

- 2 10-ounce packages broccoli spears with hollandaise sauce
- 10 to 12 large slices cooked chicken (about 1½ pounds)
- 1 10¾-ounce can cream of chicken soup
- ¼ cup skim milk
- 1 tablespoon dry sherry
- 1 tablespoon grated Parmesan cheese

Preheat oven to 425°. Prepare broccoli as directed on package. Set aside sauce pouch. Arrange broccoli in a shallow 1½-quart baking dish. Top with chicken. Combine sauce from pouch, soup, milk, and sherry. Pour over chicken and broccoli; sprinkle cheese on top. Bake for 15 to 20 minutes or until bubbly and golden brown.

Alternate cooking method: Heat in a preheated broiler, about 5 inches from heat, until bubbly and golden brown.

Chinese Chicken with Vegetables

Makes 4 servings.
Approximately 241 calories per serving.

- 2 tablespoons cornstarch
- ¼ teaspoon ground ginger
- 2 whole chicken breasts, skinned, boned, and cut into 1-inch squares
- 2 tablespoons vegetable oil
- 6 green onions, sliced diagonally
- 2 ribs celery, sliced diagonally
- 2 medium carrots, peeled and sliced diagonally
- 1 envelope beef-flavored mushroom soup mix
- 1½ cups water
- 2 tablespoons soy sauce
- 1 16-ounce can bean sprouts, drained

In a medium bowl, combine cornstarch and ginger. Toss chicken in mixture until coated. Heat 1 tablespoon of the oil in a large frying pan. Brown chicken over high heat, stirring constantly, until light brown. Remove chicken, and set aside. Add remaining oil and heat. Stir in green onions, celery, and carrots. Cook, stirring constantly, until vegetables are tender. In a small bowl, combine beef-flavored mushroom mix, water, and soy sauce; add to frying pan with chicken and bean sprouts. Cook, stirring occasionally, until heated through.

Chicken Ramekins

Makes 2 servings.
Approximately 175 calories per serving.

- 1 5-ounce can chunk-style chicken
- ¼ cup finely chopped onion
- 2 tablespoons fine dry bread crumbs
- 1 egg, lightly beaten
- 2 tablespoons unflavored, low-fat yogurt
- 1 tablespoon chopped parsley
- ¼ teaspoon grated orange rind
- ⅛ teaspoon garlic salt

Preheat oven to 350°. Thoroughly mix all ingredients together in a bowl. Pack firmly into well-buttered individual molds or 6-ounce custard cups. Bake for 30 minutes. Loosen edges; unmold.

Uncooked poultry maintains desirable flavor and texture longer in freezer storage than cooked poultry.

Chicken Breasts a la Citron
Plum Summery Salad, 16
Lo-Cal Lemon Cheesecake, 61

Apricot Chicken

Makes 8 servings.
Approximately 260 calories per serving.
Rice extra calories.

- 1 tablespoon vegetable oil
- 2½ pounds chicken, cut into serving pieces
- 2 small onions, sliced
- 1 30-ounce can apricot halves in light syrup, drained, reserve syrup
- 2 chicken bouillon cubes
- ¼ teaspoon ground ginger
- 2 tablespoons soy sauce
- 2 tablespoons cider vinegar
- ¼ cup cold water
- 1 tablespoon cornstarch
- 1 cup diagonally sliced celery
- 1 green pepper, diagonally sliced
  Cooked rice

Heat oil in a large frying pan. Brown the chicken on all sides over medium heat; set chicken aside. Sauté onions in drippings until golden; drain. Add apricot syrup and bouillon cubes; heat, stirring occasionally, until bouillon dissolves. Stir in ginger, soy sauce, and vinegar; add chicken, spooning some of the liquid over the chicken. Cover and simmer 25 to 30 minutes or until chicken is tender. Remove chicken to a warm serving platter and keep warm. Blend water and cornstarch; stir into frying pan. Simmer about 30 seconds or until mixture is thickened. Add apricots, celery and green pepper; cook about 3 minutes or until vegetables are tender-crisp. Spoon mixture over chicken. Serve with rice.

Chicken Ratatouille

Makes 4 servings.
Approximately 278 calories per serving.

- 2½ to 3 pounds chicken, cut into eighths
- 1 teaspoon salt
- ¼ teaspoon black pepper
- 1 16-ounce can tomatoes, broken up
- 1 small eggplant, cut into 3 x 1-inch fingers
- 2 small zucchini, cut into 3 x 1-inch fingers
- ½ pound fresh mushrooms, halved
- 1 bay leaf
- 2 teaspoons onion powder
- 1 teaspoon garlic powder
- 1 teaspoon crushed oregano

Preheat oven to 450°. Sprinkle salt and pepper on both sides of chicken. Place chicken, skin-side up, on a rack in a shallow roasting pan. Bake until browned, about 20 minutes. Remove chicken and the rack; drain fat. Reduce oven temperature to 350°. In the roasting pan, combine tomatoes, eggplant, zucchini, mushrooms, bay leaf, onion and garlic powders, and oregano. Place chicken on top of the vegetable mixture; spoon some of the sauce over the chicken. Cover and bake for 30 minutes. Uncover and bake until chicken is tender, about 15 minutes.

Yogurt-Baked Chicken

Makes 6 servings.
Approximately 280 calories per serving.

- 2 8-ounce cartons unflavored, low-fat yogurt
- 2 tablespoons lemon juice
- 2 tablespoons soy sauce
- 1½ teaspoons ground coriander
- ¼ teaspoon curry powder
- ¼ teaspoon black pepper
- 3 to 3½ pounds chicken, cut up

Preheat oven to 375°. Combine yogurt, lemon juice, soy sauce, coriander, curry powder, and pepper in a 3-quart baking dish. Turn chicken in sauce to coat all sides. Cover and refrigerate several hours or overnight. Bake chicken, uncovered, in sauce about 55 minutes, until tender. Baste frequently with sauce. Serve chicken in yogurt mixture.

Chicken Imperial

Makes 5 1-cup servings.
Approximately 281 calories per serving.

- 2 10-ounce packages frozen green beans, cooked and drained
- 2 cups shredded, cooked chicken
- 1 10¾-ounce can cream of mushroom soup
- 1 small can (⅔ cup) evaporated skim milk
- ¾ cup shredded process American cheese
  Dash black pepper
  Dash paprika

Preheat oven to 350°. Place green beans in a shallow, greased 1½-quart baking dish. Place chicken on top. In a saucepan, mix soup, evaporated milk, cheese, and pepper. Cook and stir over medium heat until cheese melts. Do not boil. Pour over chicken. Sprinkle paprika on top. Bake for 15 minutes or until bubbly.

Brown chicken with the skin on, but remove the skin before eating.

Chicken Honolulu

Makes 4 servings.
Approximately 250 calories per serving.

1 chicken bouillon cube
½ cup boiling water
¼ cup lemon juice
3 tablespoons soy sauce
1 tablespoon onion powder
1 teaspoon garlic powder
½ teaspoon ground ginger
¼ teaspoon black pepper
2½ pounds chicken, quartered

Preheat oven to 375°. Dissolve bouillon cube in water. Add lemon juice, soy sauce, onion powder, garlic powder, ginger, and pepper; mix well. Pour over chicken, turning to coat all sides. Cover and refrigerate 3 to 4 hours, turning once. Arrange chicken on a rack in a broiler pan. Broil until chicken is tender, about 45 minutes, turning and brushing frequently with marinade.

Pineapple Chicken Kebabs

Makes 4 servings.
Approximately 210 calories per serving.

3 whole chicken breasts (about 1 pound)
   Lively Lemon French Dressing (Recipe on page 17.)
1 green pepper, cut into chunks
1 13½-ounce can unsweetened pineapple chunks, drained
4 cups shredded iceberg lettuce

Bone and skin chicken; cut into 1-inch cubes. Marinate in half of the French Dressing for at least 4 hours. Alternately thread chicken, green pepper, and pineapple on skewers. Broil, brushing with marinade. To serve, arrange shredded lettuce on 4 dinner plates. Top with enough reserved dressing to moisten. Lay kebabs over lettuce. Serve immediately.

Roasted Chicken Feast

Makes 6 servings.
Approximately 300 calories per serving.

1 4- to 4½-pound roasting chicken
1 teaspoon salt
1 tablespoon lemon pepper
4 small potatoes, quartered
4 small onions, quartered
4 carrots, peeled and quartered
4 cups water, divided

Preheat oven to 325°. Sprinkle outside and inside of chicken with salt and lemon pepper. Stuff vegetables in cavity of chicken; truss to close. Place on a rack in a roasting pan, breast-side down. Pour 2 cups of the water in the bottom of the roaster. Water should not touch chicken. Roast for 45 minutes. Turn chicken breast-side up; add remaining 2 cups water and roast for 45 minutes or until leg moves freely when lifted and twisted.

Skillet Orange Chicken

Makes 6 servings.
Approximately 271 calories per serving.

1 tablespoon vegetable oil
2½ pounds chicken, cut into serving pieces
1 tablespoon grated orange peel
½ cup fresh orange juice
1 small onion, chopped
2 tablespoons honey
2 tablespoons water
1 orange, peeled, cut in half-cartwheels

Heat oil in a large frying pan. Fry chicken over medium heat until browned, turning frequently. Drain fat. Add orange peel, juice, onion, and honey. Cover and cook over low heat for 30 minutes or until tender. Remove chicken to a serving dish; keep warm. Gradually blend water into cooking sauce. Stir to blend and heat through. Add orange slices. Serve over chicken.

Grilled "Pickled" Chicken

Makes 8 servings.
Approximately 310 calories per serving.

2 2½-pound chickens, quartered
¼ cup margarine
1 cup garlic-flavored wine vinegar
1 tablespoon sugar
¼ cup Worcestershire sauce
1 canned jalapeno pepper
1 teaspoon dry mustard
1 small onion, minced
1 teaspoon salt

Wash and pat dry chicken. Melt margarine in a small saucepan; add remaining ingredients. Bring to a boil. Pour into a blender container; blend until smooth. Marinate chicken in sauce for about 4 hours. Prepare charcoal grill. When coals are glowing, brown chicken for 12 minutes on each side. Brush on sauce as chicken cooks; turn often. Grill until chicken is tender, 1 to 1½ hours.

Chicken with Fresh Tomato-Dill Sauce

Makes 6 servings.
Approximately 210 calories per serving.

  6 large tomatoes, peeled, seeded and chopped
  1 medium onion, chopped
  ⅓ cup chopped celery
  1 tablespoon minced fresh dill
  1½ teaspoons salt
  1 teaspoon sugar
    Dash black pepper
  2½ pounds chicken, cut into serving pieces
  1 tablespoon vegetable oil

Combine first 7 ingredients in a medium saucepan. Simmer over medium heat for 10 minutes. While sauce is simmering, brown chicken in oil in a large frying pan over medium heat; drain fat. Place chicken in a 2-quart casserole; pour sauce over chicken. Bake at 350° for 1 hour or until tender.

Piquant Chicken

Makes 6 servings.
Approximately 271 calories per serving.

  2½ pounds chicken, cut into serving pieces
  3 tablespoons lemon juice
  ½ teaspoon salt
  ¼ teaspoon black pepper
  1½ teaspoons crushed oregano
  1 16-ounce can stewed tomatoes
  1 1¼-ounce envelope onion soup mix
  ½ cup chopped green pepper
  2 tablespoons chopped onion

Preheat oven to 400°. Dip chicken in lemon juice, coating generously. Sprinkle on salt, pepper, and oregano. Place in a shallow pan. Brown in oven about 10 minutes on each side. Mix remaining ingredients; pour over chicken. Reduce heat to 350° and bake, uncovered, for 50 minutes, until tender.

Baked Mustard Chicken

Makes 10 servings.
Approximately 223 calories per serving.

  2 2½-pound chickens, quartered
  2 teaspoons salt
  ½ cup prepared mustard
  2 tablespoons vinegar
  2 tablespoons water
  1 tablespoon vegetable oil
  1 teaspoon crushed thyme
  ¼ teaspoon ground ginger

Preheat oven to 375°. Sprinkle salt on both sides of chicken. Place chicken, skin-side up, in a shallow, foil-lined baking pan. Combine mustard, vinegar, water, oil, thyme, and ginger. Spoon over chicken. Bake 50 to 60 minutes, until tender.

Salad on a Turkey Sandwich

Makes 4 servings.
Approximately 330 calories per serving.

  1 cup finely shredded lettuce
  2 medium tomatoes, finely diced
  3 green onions, thinly sliced
  1 green pepper, finely chopped
    Dash salt and black pepper
  2 tablespoons Rosy Italian Dressing (Recipe on page 17.)
  4 thin slices rye, pumpernickel or French bread
  8 slices cooked turkey breast, cut into strips
  4 slices Swiss cheese

Combine lettuce, tomatoes, onion, green pepper, salt, and pepper in a large bowl. Pour on dressing and toss lightly. Prepare sandwiches with a slice of bread, topped with turkey, Swiss cheese, and a generous portion of salad.

Lemon-Barbecued Turkey

Makes 12 servings.
Approximately 235 calories per 3½-ounce serving.

  ½ cup lemon juice
  2 tablespoons Worcestershire sauce
  2 tablespoons brown sugar
  ¼ teaspoon salt
  ¼ teaspoon garlic powder
  ¼ teaspoon dry mustard
  ¼ teaspoon paprika
  6 to 8-pound half turkey, thawed
  ¼ cup margarine

Blend all ingredients, except turkey and margarine, at least 2 hours before barbecue time. Place turkey in a large, heavy-duty plastic bag. Pour marinade over turkey and seal bag to retain marinade. Place bag in a shallow pan and refrigerate for 2 to 8 hours, turning occasionally. (Longer marinating time intensifies marinade flavor.) Remove turkey from marinade; drain. Melt margarine and add to remaining marinade. Grill in a covered barbecue or roast in a 325° oven, brushing frequently with marinade, until meat thermometer registers 180 to 185°, approximately 22 minutes per pound.

Chicken with Fresh Tomato-Dill Sauce
Stir-Fried Asparagus a la Lemon, 18

Mandarin Turkey Wings

Makes 6 servings.
Approximately 108 calories per serving.

- 2 tablespoons margarine
- 2 tablespoons vegetable oil
- 1 teaspoon paprika
- 6 turkey wings
- ¾ teaspoon salt
- ¼ teaspoon black pepper
- 4 tablespoons sesame seed, divided

Preheat oven to 350°. Melt margarine in 9 x 13-inch baking dish; stir in oil and paprika. Add turkey wings, turning once and placing skin-side down. Sprinkle on salt, pepper, and half of the sesame seed. Bake for 30 minutes. Turn wings skin-side up and sprinkle on remaining seed. Bake 30 minutes or until tender. Serve with Mandarin Sauce.

Mandarin Sauce

Makes 6 servings.
Approximately 77 calories per serving.

- 1 cup orange juice
- ½ cup low-calorie apple jelly
- 1 teaspoon lemon juice
- ¼ teaspoon ground ginger
- 1 tablespoon cornstarch
- 1 11-ounce can mandarin oranges, drained

Combine all ingredients, except oranges, in a small saucepan. Cook until smooth and clear, stirring constantly. Remove from heat. Stir in oranges.

Chinese-Broiled Turkey Steaks

Makes 6 servings.
Approximately 196 calories per serving.

- ½ cup soy sauce
- 2 tablespoons vegetable oil
- 1 tablespoon honey
- ⅛ teaspoon ground ginger
- 1 teaspoon dry mustard
- 3 cloves garlic, minced
- 1½ pounds turkey breast steaks, ¾ to 1 inch thick

Combine all ingredients, except turkey. Pour over turkey steaks. Cover and refrigerate for several hours or overnight. Drain turkey. Cook on both sides over hot coals or in a broiler, 6 to 8 minutes on each side. Brush occasionally with remaining marinade, if desired.

Curried Pineapple Turkey Breast Roast

Makes 8 servings.
Approximately 195 calories per 3½-ounce serving.

- 4 to 6 pound turkey breast, thawed

Preheat oven to 325°. Place turkey breast skin-side up on a rack in a shallow roasting pan. (If a meat thermometer is used, insert into the center of the breast, away from the bone.) Roast until meat thermometer registers 170°, approximately 22 minutes per pound or refer to the chart on the turkey breast wrapper. During the last 10 to 15 minutes of roasting, spoon Curried Pineapple Glaze over turkey.

Curried Pineapple Glaze

- 2 teaspoons cornstarch
- 1 teaspoon curry powder
- ¼ teaspoon onion salt
- ⅛ teaspoon garlic powder
- 2 tablespoons cold water
- 1 8¾-ounce can crushed pineapple in unsweetened juice
- 2 tablespoons brown sugar
- 1 tablespoon margarine

Combine first 4 ingredients; mix lightly. Stir in cold water. In a saucepan, heat pineapple, brown sugar, and margarine; add cornstarch mixture. Cook and stir over low heat until smooth and clear.

Turkey Bunwiches

Makes 6 servings.
Approximately 296 calories per serving.

- 2 cups coarsely-diced, cooked turkey
- ½ cup diced celery
- 2 tablespoons chopped chives or onion
- ½ cup diced Cheddar cheese
- 1 teaspoon chopped pimiento
- 2 hard-cooked eggs, chopped
- ½ cup reduced calorie mayonnaise
  Salt and pepper to taste
- 6 hamburger buns
  Olives, pickles, carrot curls, optional

Preheat oven to 400°. Combine turkey, celery, chives, cheese, pimiento, and eggs. Add mayonnaise; season with salt and pepper. Slice top off each bun and scoop out center. Fill hollows with turkey mixture. Replace bun tops and wrap each sandwich in foil. Heat for 15 to 20 minutes. Garnish top of each bun with olive, pickle, and carrot curl, speared with a toothpick.

Sweet and Sour Turkey Drums

Makes 8 servings.
Approximately 340 calories per serving.

- ½ cup flour
- ¼ teaspoon salt
- ¼ teaspoon paprika
- Dash black pepper
- 4 turkey drumsticks
- 3 tablespoons vegetable oil
- 1 medium onion, chopped
- 1½ cups water
- ¾ cup catsup
- ½ cup cider vinegar
- 1 tablespoon honey
- ¼ teaspoon ground cloves
- ½ teaspoon cinnamon

Combine flour, salt, paprika, and pepper. Coat drumsticks with seasoned flour. Heat oil in a large frying pan or Dutch oven. Brown turkey on all sides. Drain excess oil. Add onion and sauté until tender. Add water, catsup, vinegar, honey, and spices. Bring to a boil. Reduce heat, cover, and simmer 1½ hours or until tender.

Turkey Corn Pudding

Makes 6 servings.
Approximately 250 calories per serving.

- 6 large slices or 2 cups diced, cooked turkey
- 1 4-ounce can sliced mushrooms, drained
- ¼ cup margarine
- ¼ cup flour
- ½ teaspoon salt
- ¼ teaspoon black pepper
- 1 cup skim milk
- ¼ teaspoon Worcestershire sauce
- 2 eggs, separated
- 1 8¾-ounce can cream-style corn

Preheat oven to 350°. Arrange turkey and mushrooms in a 1½-quart casserole or baking dish sprayed with vegetable spray; set aside. Melt margarine in a saucepan. Stir in flour, salt, and pepper. Gradually add milk. Stir constantly over medium heat until sauce thickens. Combine Worcestershire sauce with egg yolks; beat lightly with fork. Blend a little of the hot mixture into the egg yolks; then stir into pudding. Cook 2 minutes. Remove from heat. Stir in corn. Beat egg whites until stiff but not dry. Gently fold into corn mixture until whites disappear. Pour over turkey and mushrooms. Bake for 30 to 40 minutes until lightly browned.

Skillet Turkey Cutlets Parmesan

Makes 4 servings.
Approximately 333 calories per serving.

- 1½ teaspoons lemon juice
- 1 pound turkey breast steaks, ⅜ to ½ inch thick
- 2 tablespoons flour
- ½ teaspoon salt
- Dash black pepper
- 1 egg
- 1 teaspoon water
- ½ cup cornflake crumbs
- ½ cup shredded Parmesan cheese
- 2 tablespoons margarine
- Lemon slices, optional
- Fresh basil sprigs, optional

Drizzle lemon juice over steaks. Combine flour, salt, and pepper. Mix together egg and water. Combine cornflake crumbs and cheese. Dip steaks in seasoned flour; shake off excess. Dip in egg; allow excess to run off. Roll in crumbs. Heat margarine in a large frying pan. Cook steaks about 2 minutes on each side, until golden brown and cooked through. Garnish with lemon slices and fresh basil sprigs.

Turkey Chow Mein

Makes 6 servings.
Approximately 171 calories per serving.
½ cup chow mein noodles, approximately 105 calories.

- 1 tablespoon margarine
- 1 green pepper, seeded and julienned
- 1 cup sliced celery
- 1¾ cups chicken broth
- 2 tablespoons cornstarch
- ¼ cup cold water
- 2 tablespoons soy sauce
- ½ envelope onion soup mix
- 2 cups diced, cooked turkey
- 1 4-ounce can sliced mushrooms, drained
- 1 5-ounce can sliced water chestnuts, drained
- 1 16-ounce can bean sprouts, drained
- Chow mein noodles

Heat margarine in a large frying pan. Sauté green pepper and celery for 2 minutes. Add chicken broth. Blend cornstarch with cold water and soy sauce; gradually stir into the broth. Add onion soup mix. Cook and stir until mixture thickens and bubbles. Add turkey, mushrooms, water chestnuts, and bean sprouts; heat. Serve over chow mein noodles.

Pork, Veal, Lamb

Coriander Pork Chops

Makes 4 servings.
Approximately 349 calories per serving.

- 2 cloves garlic, crushed
- 1 tablespoon crushed coriander seed
- 8 black peppercorns, crushed
- 1 teaspoon brown sugar
- 3 tablespoons soy sauce
- 4 loin pork chops, 1½ inches thick

Combine all ingredients, except pork chops; mix lightly. Brush chops with marinade. Cover and set aside for 30 minutes, brushing occasionally with marinade. Place chops on a grill; reserve marinade. Grill over moderate heat for 10 to 12 minutes per side, or until thoroughly cooked, brushing occasionally with marinade.

Pork Jambalaya

Makes 6 servings.
Approximately 326 calories per serving.

- 1 pound lean, boneless pork shoulder, cut into narrow strips
  Salt and pepper
- 1 tablespoon vegetable oil
- 1 cup chopped celery
- 1 cup chopped green pepper
- 1 cup sliced green onions with tops
- 1 cup uncooked rice
- 2½ cups chicken broth
- 1 teaspoon garlic salt
  Dash cayenne pepper, optional

Preheat oven to 375°. Season pork with salt and pepper to taste. Heat oil in an ovenproof frying pan. Add celery, green pepper, and onion. Sauté until tender. Stir in rice, broth, and seasonings. Bring to a boil. Cover and bake for 30 to 35 minutes or until rice is tender and liquid is absorbed. Fluff rice with a fork.

Smoked Pork with Potato-Kraut

Makes 8 servings.
Approximately 329 calories per serving.

- 1 2-pound smoked pork shoulder roll
- 2 cups water
- 4 large red potatoes, pared and halved
- 3 small onions, quartered
- 1 27-ounce can sauerkraut, drained
  Dash black pepper, optional

Place pork shoulder in a Dutch oven. Add water; cover tightly and cook slowly for 90 minutes. Add potatoes and onion; cover and cook for 30 minutes or until meat and vegetables are tender. Add sauerkraut and pepper; heat through. Carve meat; serve with the vegetables.

Porkebabs Italienne

Makes 6 servings.
Approximately 323 calories per serving.

- 2 pounds boneless pork shoulder, cut into 1- to 1¼-inch cubes
- 1 8-ounce bottle lite Italian-style salad dressing
- 2 small zucchini squash
- 12 cherry tomatoes

Combine pork cubes and salad dressing; refrigerate for 4 hours or overnight. Cut squash in 1-inch diagonal pieces. Alternately thread 4 12-inch metal skewers with pork cubes, zucchini, and cherry tomatoes. Brush with marinade. Broil kebabs as far as possible from heat for 30 minutes or until well done, turning occasionally.

Oriental Pork

Makes 8 servings.
Approximately 248 calories per serving.

- 2 pounds lean ground pork
- ½ teaspoon salt
- 2 tablespoons cornstarch
- ¼ teaspoon ground ginger
- ½ cup water
- 1 13¼-ounce can chunk pineapple in unsweetened juice, drained, reserve juice
- ⅓ cup soy sauce
- 1 clove garlic, crushed
- 2 medium green peppers, cut into strips
- 1 8-ounce can sliced water chestnuts
- 2 tablespoons chopped green onion

Lightly brown ground pork in a large frying pan; drain fat. Sprinkle salt over meat. Combine cornstarch and ginger; blend in water; add to meat. Stir reserved pineapple juice, soy sauce, and garlic into meat mixture. Cover and cook slowly for 20 minutes, stirring occasionally. Stir in pineapple, green peppers, water chestnuts, and onion. Cover and cook for 5 minutes or until vegetables are tender-crisp.

Veal-Olive Birds

Makes 6 servings.
Approximately 308 calories per serving.

- 2 pounds veal round steak, cut ½ inch thick or 6 veal cutlets
- ⅓ cup chopped, stuffed olives
- ⅓ cup chopped pecans
- ⅓ cup chopped celery
- 1 tablespoon vegetable oil
- ½ teaspoon salt
- ½ teaspoon paprika
- 1 10¾-ounce can cream of mushroom soup
- ½ cup skim milk

Cut veal steak into 6 pieces. Pound to ¼-inch thickness. Combine olives, pecans, and celery; mix lightly. Place an equal amount of olive mixture on each piece of meat. Roll up and fasten with toothpicks or tie with string. Heat oil in a heavy frying pan. Brown veal; drain fat. Sprinkle salt and paprika over veal. Combine mushroom soup and milk; mix well. Add to meat; cover tightly and cook for 45 minutes or until meat is done.

Veal Delight

Makes 6 servings.
Approximately 283 calories per serving.

- 1 tablespoon vegetable oil
- 6 veal chops, ¾ inch thick (about 2 pounds)
  Salt and pepper
- 1 chicken bouillon cube
- ½ cup boiling water
- ½ cup dry white wine
- 1 tablespoon cornstarch
- ¼ cup water
- 1 tablespoon snipped parsley
- 1 tablespoon chopped green onion
- 1 cup halved and seeded Tokay or green grapes
- 2 teaspoons lemon juice

Heat oil in a heavy frying pan. Brown chops in oil. Season with salt and pepper to taste. Dissolve bouillon in boiling water; add to chops along with the wine. Cover and simmer for 45 to 55 minutes or until meat is tender. Remove chops to a warm platter. Skim fat from wine mixture. Combine cornstarch and the ¼ cup water; stir into wine mixture. Add parsley and green onion. Cook over medium heat until mixture is thickened and bubbly, stirring constantly. Stir in grapes and lemon juice; heat through. To serve, pour sauce over chops.

Veal and Spinach Rolls

Makes 6 servings.
Approximately 295 calories per serving.

- 2 veal round steaks, cut ½ inch thick (about 2 pounds)
- 2 slices bacon, diced
- ¼ cup chopped onion
- 2 cups chopped spinach
- ¾ cup cooked rice
- ½ teaspoon salt
- ¼ teaspoon garlic salt
  Dash black pepper
- ⅛ teaspoon marjoram
- ⅛ teaspoon ground nutmeg
- 1 tablespoon vegetable oil
- 1 8-ounce can tomato sauce
- ¼ cup water

Cut veal into 6 serving-size pieces; pound to about ¼-inch thickness. Sauté bacon and onion in a heavy frying pan until lightly browned. Add spinach, rice, salt, garlic salt, pepper, marjoram, and nutmeg. Stir over low heat until spinach is slightly wilted. Place approximately 2 tablespoons spinach stuffing on each piece of veal. Roll up jelly-roll fashion; fasten with toothpicks. Heat oil in a heavy frying pan. Add veal; brown well. Drain fat. Combine tomato sauce and water; pour over veal. Cover tightly and cook slowly for 45 to 60 minutes or until meat is cooked.

Veal Italian

Makes 5 servings.
Approximately 280 calories per serving.
Rice or noodles extra calories.

- 1 pound veal round steak, ¼ inch thick
- 1 teaspoon salt
- ¼ teaspoon white pepper
- ¼ teaspoon thyme
- 2 tablespoons vegetable oil
- 1 small clove garlic
- ⅔ cup white cooking wine
- 1 16-ounce can sliced carrots, drained
- 14 cherry tomatoes, halved
  Chopped parsley

Cut veal into 2-inch pieces; sprinkle on salt, pepper, and thyme. Heat oil in a large frying pan. Add veal and garlic and sauté until meat is browned. Discard garlic. Add wine. Cover and simmer for 20 minutes. Add carrots and tomatoes; simmer 10 minutes, until meat is tender. Sprinkle on parsley. Serve over rice or noodles.

Teriyaki Lamb Chops

Makes 4 servings.
Approximately 319 calories per serving.

    8 lean lamb rib chops, cut ¾ inch thick, fat trimmed
    ¾ cup water
    ⅓ cup soy sauce
    1 teaspoon ground ginger
    ¼ teaspoon black pepper
    2 teaspoons sugar
    1 green pepper, cut into strips
    1 clove garlic, minced
    1 cup diagonally sliced celery
    1 8-ounce can sliced water chestnuts, drained
    1 6-ounce package frozen pea pods
    1 tablespoon cornstarch
    ¼ cup dry sherry

Heat a large, heavy frying pan. Place chops in the pan and brown on each side. Remove from heat. In a small bowl, mix together water, soy sauce, ginger, pepper, and sugar. Return lamb to heat. Pour on sauce. Cover and simmer for about 30 minutes, or until lamb is tender. Add green pepper, garlic, celery, and water chestnuts. Simmer about 10 minutes, or until vegetables are tender-crisp. Add pea pods. Combine cornstarch and sherry; mix well. Add to lamb and vegetables. Simmer until sauce thickens slightly.

Lamb Kebabs

Makes 6 servings.
Approximately 275 calories per serving.

    1 or 2 green peppers, cut into 1- to 1½-inch squares
    4 ribs celery, cut into 1- to 1½-inch squares
    3 large carrots, cut into 1-inch pieces
    ½ pound fresh mushrooms
    1½ pounds lean lamb, cut into ¾-inch cubes
    1½ teaspoons salt
      Dash black pepper
    3 cups tomato sauce
    ¾ teaspoon whole cloves
      Dash crushed oregano
    2 tablespoons Worcestershire sauce

Preheat oven to 325°. Parboil green peppers, celery, carrots, and mushrooms for 10 minutes. Alternately thread meat and vegetables on skewers. Place skewers in a single layer in a roasting pan. Sprinkle on salt and pepper. Combine tomato sauce, cloves, oregano, and Worcestershire sauce; pour over kebabs. Bake for 30 to 45 minutes, or until meat is tender. Baste frequently with pan liquid.

Lamb Burgers

Makes 6 servings.
Approximately 363 calories per serving.

    2 pounds lean ground lamb
    ½ cup minced green pepper
    ¼ cup soy sauce
    2 teaspoons grated lemon rind
    ½ teaspoon ground ginger
    6 unsweetened pineapple slices
    6 tablespoons plain low-fat yogurt

Gently mix together lamb, green pepper, soy sauce, lemon rind, and ginger. Shape into 12 patties, slightly larger in diameter than the pineapple slices. Top 6 of the patties with a pineapple slice; spoon 1 tablespoon of yogurt into the center of each. Top the pineapple with another lamb pattie; pinch the edges together all the way round to form a large burger. Grill about 4 inches above coals for 6 to 8 minutes per side or to desired doneness.

Low-Cal Lamb Casserole

Makes 6 servings.
Approximately 252 calories per serving.

    1½ pounds boneless leg of lamb, fat trimmed and cut into thin slices
    1 cup thinly sliced potatoes
    1 cup thinly sliced carrots
    1 eggplant, peeled and diced
    1 cup sliced celery
      Salt and pepper
    1 cup sliced yellow or zucchini squash
    1 cup sliced onion
    1 cup lima beans
    1 cup sliced tomatoes
    1 10½-ounce can beef bouillon
    ¼ teaspoon Tabasco sauce
    1 clove garlic, minced
    1 teaspoon dried dillweed

Place lamb on aluminum foil and broil until lightly browned on both sides. In a 3½-quart casserole, arrange a layer each of potatoes, carrots, eggplant, and celery. Sprinkle on salt and pepper to taste. Arrange half of the lamb in a layer, then layer squash, onion, lima beans, and remaining lamb slices; sprinkle each layer with salt and pepper. Top with sliced tomato. Mix together bouillon, Tabasco sauce, garlic, and dillweed. Pour over all. Cover and bake at 350° for 1 hour, or until lamb and vegetables are tender.

Stuffed Sole Supreme

Makes 8 servings.
Approximately 274 calories per serving.

    3 cups diced tomatoes
2½ cups sliced celery
1½ cups diced onion
    ½ cup diced green pepper
    1 cup chicken broth
    1 8-ounce can tomato sauce
    2 tablespoons vegetable oil
    1 teaspoon Italian seasoning
    1 clove garlic, minced
    ½ teaspoon salt
    ½ teaspoon sugar
      Dash black pepper
    1 6-ounce can sliced mushrooms
2½ cups dried bread crumbs
1½ pounds sole fillets

Preheat oven to 375°. In a saucepan, combine tomatoes, 2 cups of the celery, ¾ cup of the onion, green pepper, broth, tomato sauce, 1 tablespoon of the oil, and seasonings. Bring to a boil; reduce heat, cover and simmer about 45 minutes, stirring often. Add more broth, if sauce becomes too thick. Drain mushrooms; reserve liquid and ¼ cup of the mushrooms for the stuffing. Add remaining mushrooms to sauce. In a frying pan, heat remaining 1 tablespoon oil. Add remaining ½ cup celery, and ¾ cup onion; sauté until onion is lightly browned. Add reserved mushrooms and bread crumbs. Add enough reserved mushroom liquid to make stuffing as moist as desired. Place a spoonful of the stuffing on each fillet; roll up firmly and secure ends with toothpicks. Arrange in a shallow casserole. Pour tomato sauce over fish. Bake, uncovered, for 20 to 25 minutes. Serve with the tomato sauce from the casserole.

Tuna Aubergines

Makes 6 servings.
Approximately 220 calories per serving.

    1 eggplant, sliced
    2 medium tomatoes, sliced
    1 teaspoon salt
    2 6½- to 7-ounce cans tuna, packed in water, drained and flaked
1½ teaspoons crushed basil
    ¼ cup chopped onion
    ½ pound skim milk mozzarella cheese, shredded

Preheat oven to 350°. Arrange overlapping slices of eggplant and tomato in a buttered, 2-quart casserole dish. Sprinkle on salt. Combine tuna, basil, and onion; mix lightly. Place tuna in the center of the eggplant and tomato slices. Top with cheese. Bake for 45 to 50 minutes.

Confetti Fish Rolls

Makes 6 servings.
Approximately 135 calories per serving.

1½ pounds sole or flounder fillets
      Salt and pepper
    1 small tomato, diced
    2 tablespoons minced green pepper
    2 slices American cheese, diced
    1 tablespoon Worcestershire sauce
      Paprika

Preheat oven to 350°. Lightly season each fillet with salt and pepper. Combine tomato, green pepper, cheese, and Worcestershire sauce; place a spoonful on each fillet. Roll up and place, seam-side down, in a shallow baking dish. Sprinkle on paprika. Bake for 20 minutes or until fish flakes easily.

Fish au Poivre

Makes 4 servings.
Approximately 115 calories per serving.

    1 pound sole or flounder fillets
    2 teaspoons margarine
    ½ cup shredded carrot
    ½ cup diced, fresh mushrooms
    1 tablespoon grated lemon peel
    1 teaspoon onion powder
    ½ teaspoon salt
    ¼ teaspoon black pepper
    ¼ teaspoon crushed marjoram
      Lemon wedges, optional

Preheat oven to 350°. Brush 1 side of each fillet with margarine. Combine remaining ingredients; mix well. Spoon mixture onto the center of the buttered side of each fillet. Roll up fillet; place seam-side down in a lightly greased baking pan. Bake, uncovered, until fish flakes easily when tested with a fork, about 25 minutes. Garnish with lemon wedges.

Baked Fish Steaks a la Crecy

Makes 4 servings.
Approximately 166 calories per serving.

- 1 pound halibut steaks, 1 inch thick
- 3 tablespoons fresh lemon juice
- Salt
- Paprika
- 1 tablespoon margarine
- ½ cup plain low-fat yogurt
- ¼ cup shredded carrot
- ¼ cup shredded, peeled cucumber, well drained
- 1 tablespoon sliced green onion
- 1 teaspoon grated lemon peel
- Dash seasoned salt
- Lemon wedges, optional
- Parsley sprigs, optional

Preheat oven to 450°. Place fish on a large piece of heavy duty aluminum foil. Sprinkle with 2 tablespoons of the lemon juice, and salt and paprika to taste. Dot with margarine. Wrap securely in foil; place on baking sheet. Bake for 12 to 14 minutes, until fish flakes easily. Make sauce by combining the yogurt, carrot, cucumber, green onion, lemon peel, seasoned salt, and remaining lemon juice. Serve with fish. Garnish with lemon wedges and parsley.

Tuna-Lentil Creole

Makes 6 servings.
Approximately 284 calories per serving. Rice extra calories.

- 1 cup dried lentils
- 2½ teaspoons salt, divided
- 1 tablespoon butter or margarine
- 2 cups chopped green pepper
- ¾ cup chopped onion
- 1 10-ounce package frozen, sliced okra, thawed
- 1 28-ounce can tomatoes
- 1 teaspoon sugar
- ⅛ teaspoon Tabasco sauce
- 2 6½- or 7-ounce cans tuna, packed in water, drained and flaked
- Cooked rice

Place lentils in a medium saucepan; cover with water; add 2 teaspoons of the salt. Bring to a boil. Cook over medium heat for 1½ hours; add more water, if needed. Drain and set aside. Melt butter in large saucepan. Add green pepper, onion, and okra; cook 2 to 3 minutes. Add tomatoes, sugar, Tabasco, remaining ½ teaspoon salt and lentils. Cover; simmer 30 minutes. Add tuna; simmer 10 minutes. Serve over hot rice.

Rock Lobster Continental

Makes 4 servings.
Approximately 260 calories per serving.

- 20 ounces cooked rock lobster tail meat
- 2 10-ounce packages frozen, chopped spinach, thawed and squeezed dry
- Salt, pepper, onion, and garlic powder
- 8 ounces cottage cheese
- 1 beef bouillon cube, dissolved in ½ cup water
- ½ cup tomato juice
- 1 cup fresh, sliced mushrooms
- Salt and pepper

Preheat oven to 350°. Slice lobster meat into medallions. In a bowl, season spinach to taste with salt, pepper, onion, and garlic powders. Divide spinach into 4 scallop shells or baking dishes. Spoon lobster over top of spinach mixture. In a saucepan, combine cottage cheese, bouillon, and tomato juice. Add mushrooms; stir over low heat until sauce bubbles. Season to taste with salt and pepper. Spoon sauce over lobster. Bake for 10 minutes or until piping hot.

Baked Fish Supreme

Makes 8 servings.
Approximately 197 calories per serving.

- 2 pounds haddock fillets, ¾ inch thick
- 2 grapefruit
- 1 teaspoon salt
- ¼ teaspoon black pepper
- 3 tablespoons melted margarine
- 1 10¾-ounce can cream of asparagus soup
- ½ cup dairy sour cream
- 3 green onions, thinly sliced
- 1 tablespoon chopped parsley

Cut the fish into serving pieces. Place in a shallow baking pan. Peel and section grapefruit over a bowl to retain juices. Drain sections. Pour juice over fish. Marinate at room temperature for 10 to 15 minutes; drain juice. Sprinkle salt and pepper on fish. Pour half of the margarine over the fish. Broil 4 inches from heat for about 5 minutes. Baste with remaining margarine and broil 3 to 5 minutes, until fish is slightly browned. Remove from broiler and baste with pan juices. Cool slightly. Combine soup with sour cream, green onions, and parsley. Spoon over fish. Top with grapefruit sections. Bake at 350° for 10 to 15 minutes, or until heated through.

Lobster Newburg

Makes 4 servings.
Approximately 261 calories per serving. If served over toast, add 44 calories per slice.

    1 cup evaporated skim milk
    2 ounces Gruyere cheese, cubed
    1 egg
    ½ teaspoon bitters
    1 cup sliced mushrooms
    2 tablespoons chopped chives
   18 ounces cooked rock lobster, sliced
      Salt and pepper

Pour skim milk into saucepan. Gradually stir in cheese, egg, and bitters. Stir in mushrooms and chives. Stir over low heat until sauce bubbles and thickens. Stir in lobster. Season to taste with salt and pepper. Heat until bubbly. Spoon lobster and sauce over diet toast.

South African Rarebit

Makes 6 servings.
Approximately 225 calories per serving. Add 44 calories per slice of toast.

   1⅔ cups evaporated skim milk
    2 tablespoons tomato sauce
    8 ounces sharp Cheddar cheese, coarsely grated
    ¼ teaspoon crushed basil
    ½ teaspoon salt
   20 ounces cooked rock lobster meat, diced
    6 pieces diet toast

In a saucepan, combine evaporated milk and to-mato sauce. Slowly heat until bubbles appear around the edge of the pan. Gradually add cheese. Stir until cheese is melted and sauce is smooth and thick. Add basil and salt and blend well. Keep sauce warm in a chafing dish. To serve, divide lobster among toast and spoon sauce over all.

Broiled Scallops

Makes 2 servings.
Approximately 195 calories per serving.

    ¼ cup chicken bouillon
    ½ teaspoon imitation butter flavoring
    2 teaspoons lemon juice
    1 teaspoon grated lemon rind
    ⅛ teaspoon bitters
    ⅛ teaspoon ground ginger
    ⅛ teaspoon chili powder
    1 pound scallops

Combine chicken bouillon, imitation butter fla-voring, lemon juice, lemon rind, bitters, ginger, and chili powder. Brush over scallops. Broil about 3 inches from heat for 5 minutes or until scallops are cooked through. Brush with bouillon mixture once during broiling and again before serving.

Seaside Casserole

Makes 6 servings.
Approximately 237 calories per serving. Chow mein noodles extra calories.

    1 medium onion, chopped
    1 tablespoon margarine, melted
    1 10¾-ounce can cream of shrimp soup
    1 8-ounce can water chestnuts, drained and sliced
    ½ cup skim milk
    ½ cup sour half and half
    2 6½-ounce cans water-packed, chunk tuna, drained and flaked
    1 17-ounce can peas, drained
      Salt and pepper
      Chow mein noodles

Sauté onion in margarine until tender. Stir in next 5 ingredients; bring mixture to a boil. Gently fold in peas; salt and pepper to taste. Heat to serving temperature and serve over chow mein noodles.

Tuna Ratatouille

Makes 6 servings.
Approximately 186 calories per serving.

    2 tablespoons margarine
    1 clove garlic, mashed
    2 medium onions, thinly sliced
    2 small zucchini, sliced
    1 small eggplant, cubed
    1 teaspoon salt
    ¼ teaspoon black pepper
    ½ teaspoon crushed oregano
    1 15-ounce can tomato sauce with bits
    2 6½-ounce cans tuna, packed in water, drained and flaked

Heat margarine in a large frying pan. Add garlic and onion; sauté until onion is tender. Layer remaining vegetables in pan, sprinkling each layer with salt, pepper, and oregano. Add tomato sauce. Cover and simmer for 15 minutes. Add tuna and cook until vegetables are tender.

Eggplant Stuffed with Tuna

Makes 4 servings.
Approximately 274 calories per serving.

- 2 tablespoons margarine
- ¼ cup chopped green pepper
- ¼ cup chopped onion
- 2 medium eggplants
- 2 teaspoons lemon juice
- 1¼ teaspoons salt
- ¼ teaspoon pepper
- 2 medium tomatoes, peeled and chopped
- 2 tablespoons chopped parsley
- ¼ teaspoon dried leaf oregano
- ¼ teaspoon basil
- 2 6½- or 7-ounce cans tuna, packed in water, drained and flaked
- 1 cup buttered, soft bread crumbs

Melt margarine in a frying pan. Sauté green pepper and onion until tender. Cut a thin, lengthwise slice from each eggplant. Remove pulp, leaving a ¼-inch thick shell; dice pulp. Add eggplant, lemon juice, salt, pepper, tomatoes, parsley, and herbs to frying pan. Cook until eggplant is tender, about 5 minutes. Add tuna; toss together. Spoon into shells. Place shells in a pan filled with ¼-inch water. Bake at 400° for 20 minutes. Remove from oven; top with crumbs. Bake until crumbs are golden.

Salmon Rolls

Makes 6 servings.
Approximately 138 calories per serving.

- 1 egg, lightly beaten
- ¼ cup minced onion
- 1 teaspoon Worcestershire sauce
  Salt and pepper
- 1 16-ounce can pink salmon, drained, flaked, and bones removed
- ¾ cup cooked rice
- 6 large cabbage leaves
  Cheese Sauce (Recipe on page 53)
  Paprika

Preheat oven to 350°. Combine first 3 ingredients, and salt and pepper to taste. Add salmon and rice; mix well. Immerse cabbage in boiling water until limp, 2 to 3 minutes; drain. Slit the heavy center vein of cabbage 2 inches up the leaf. Place ⅓ cup salmon mixture on each leaf; fold in sides and tuck ends under. Place seamside down in a sprayed, shallow baking dish. Cover with foil; bake for 45 minutes. Serve with Cheese Sauce; garnish with paprika.

Apple-Tuna Mousse

Makes 6 servings.
Approximately 95 calories per serving.

- 1 3-ounce package low-calorie, lemon-flavored gelatin
- ¼ teaspoon salt
  Dash black pepper
- 1 cup boiling water
- 1 tablespoon lemon juice
- 1 5.33-ounce can evaporated milk
- 1 cup finely chopped Red or Golden Delicious apple
- 1 7-ounce can tuna, packed in water, drained and flaked
- ½ cup sliced ripe olives
- 2 tablespoons chopped chives
  Salad greens
  Red or Golden Delicious apple slices

Place gelatin, salt, and pepper in a bowl. Add water and stir until gelatin is dissolved. Stir in lemon juice. Chill until syrupy. Chill evaporated milk in a freezer tray until partially frozen. Place in a mixing bowl; whip until stiff peaks form. Add apple, tuna, olives, and chives to gelatin. Fold gelatin mixture into whipped milk. Turn into a 6-cup mold. Chill until set. Unmold on a plate lined with salad greens and garnish with apple slices.

Lobster Thermidor

Makes 5 servings.
Approximately 288 calories per serving.

- 5 5-ounce frozen rock lobster tails
- 4 ounces cottage cheese
- 3 tablespoons buttermilk
- 1 teaspoon dry mustard
- ½ teaspoon Worcestershire sauce
- 1 teaspoon salt
- 2 teaspoons paprika
- 1 tablespoon minced parsley
- ½ tablespoon lemon juice
- 5 ounces Swiss cheese, grated

Preheat oven to 400°. Parboil frozen lobster tails by dropping into boiling, salted water. When water returns to a boil, drain lobster and drench with cold water. Cut away underside membrane; pull out meat and dice; reserve shells. Combine all ingredients, except Swiss cheese; mix well. Spoon mixture into the 5 shells. Top each with Swiss cheese. Bake for 10 minutes or until cheese melts.

Cook more fish than you need for one meal. Use leftover fish chopped up in a salad.

Fish Steaks Emperor

Makes 3 servings.
Approximately 193 calories per serving.

  3 tablespoons soy sauce
⅛ teaspoon ground ginger
  1 teaspoon sugar
  2 to 3 cod steaks (about 1½ pounds)
  2 tablespoons chopped parsley

Preheat oven to 400°. Combine soy sauce, ginger, and sugar. Place fish in a pan. Pour on marinade; let stand 30 minutes. Bake for about 15 minutes, until fish flakes easily. Sprinkle on parsley before serving.

Fiesta Shrimp and Rice

Makes 6 servings.
Approximately 201 calories per serving.

  2 tablespoons margarine
  2 tablespoons instant minced onion
½ teaspoon minced garlic
  1 bay leaf
  1 cup uncooked rice
  1 4-ounce can mushrooms, drained
  1 chicken bouillon cube
2½ cups water
  1 10-ounce package frozen peas
  2 4½-ounce cans shrimp, rinsed and drained

Melt margarine over medium heat. Add all ingredients, except peas and shrimp. Bring to a boil; reduce heat, cover and simmer for 15 minutes. Add peas and shrimp and simmer for 15 minutes.

Shrimp Perfection Aspic

Makes 6 servings.
Approximately 50 calories per serving.

¼ cup sweet pepper flakes
¼ cup celery flakes
  2 teaspoons instant minced onion
⅓ cup water
  1 envelope unflavored gelatin
¼ cup cold water
  1 cup tomato juice
  1 cup clam juice
  1 tablespoon lemon juice
  1 teaspoon salt
½ teaspoon crushed oregano
¼ teaspoon black pepper
¼ teaspoon garlic powder
  1 4½-ounce can shrimp, drained
    Salad greens, optional

Combine pepper and celery flakes, minced onion, and ⅓ cup water; let stand 10 minutes to rehydrate. Soften gelatin in the ¼ cup cold water. Heat tomato juice and add to gelatin. Stir in clam and lemon juices, seasonings, and rehydrated vegetables. Chill until the mixture begins to thicken. Fold in shrimp. Turn into a 1-quart mold rinsed in cold water. Chill until firm. Unmold onto a serving plate lined with salad greens.

Haddock Almondine

Makes 5 servings.
Approximately 188 calories per serving.

  3 tablespoons unsalted margarine
¼ cup sliced almonds
1¼ pounds haddock fillets
½ teaspoon crushed basil
¼ teaspoon black pepper
    Lemon wedges
    Parsley sprigs

In a saucepan, melt 1 tablespoon of the margarine. Add sliced almonds and stir over medium heat for 2 or 3 minutes; set aside. Place haddock skin-side down on broiler rack; dot with remaining margarine. Sprinkle on basil and pepper. Place 2 inches from heat and broil for 9 minutes. Sprinkle almonds on top and broil about 3 minutes, or until fish flakes easily. Fish does not need to be turned. Remove to a serving platter. Garnish with lemon wedges and parsley sprigs.

Broiled Rock Lobster Tails

Makes 4 servings.
Approximately 134 calories per serving.

  4 5-ounce rock lobster tails
¼ cup chicken bouillon
  2 to 3 drops imitation butter flavoring
  2 teaspoons lemon juice
  1 teaspoon minced, dried orange rind
⅛ teaspoon bitters
⅛ teaspoon ground ginger
⅛ teaspoon chili powder

Cut lengthwise through tops of shells to keep lobster tails from curling while cooking. Place lobsters on a broiler pan, meat-side up. Combine bouillon, butter flavoring, lemon juice, orange rind, bitters, ginger, and chili powder. Brush over lobster. Broil about 4 inches from heat for 8 to 10 minutes.

Haddock Elegante

Makes 5 servings.
Approximately 130 calories per serving.

- 1 pound haddock fillets
- ½ teaspoon salt
  Dash black pepper
- 2 tomatoes, peeled and sliced
- ¼ cup dry white wine
- ½ teaspoon crushed basil
- ½ cup shredded sharp process American cheese

Preheat oven to 350°. Place fillets in a shallow, greased baking dish. Sprinkle on ¼ teaspoon of the salt and the pepper. Arrange tomatoes on top; sprinkle on remaining salt. Carefully pour wine over all; sprinkle on basil. Bake for 20 minutes. Sprinkle on cheese; bake 5 to 10 minutes or until fish flakes easily.

Fish Creole

Makes 4 servings.
Approximately 176 calories per serving.

- 1 pound haddock, cod or halibut fillets
- 1 tablespoon margarine
- 1 8-ounce can stewed tomatoes, cut into pieces
- ¼ cup chopped onion
- ¼ cup minced celery
- 2 tablespoons chopped green pepper
- 1 tablespoon sugar
- ¾ teaspoon salt
- ¼ teaspoon crushed oregano
  Dash black pepper

Preheat oven to 350°. Rinse fillets and pat dry with a towel. Arrange in a shallow baking dish. Melt margarine in a medium saucepan. Stir in remaining ingredients; mix well. Carefully pour tomato mixture over fish. Bake for about 35 minutes, until fish flakes easily.

Halibut Superb

Makes 2 servings.
Approximately 310 calories per serving.

- ¼ teaspoon mace
- ½ teaspoon bitters
- ½ cup skim milk
- 2 10-ounce halibut steaks

Preheat oven to 400°. Combine mace, bitters, and skim milk. Place fish in a shallow baking dish. Pour milk mixture over fish. Bake for 15 minutes or until fish flakes easily.

Baked Orange Halibut

Makes 4 servings.
Approximately 142 calories per serving.

- 1 pound halibut fillets
- 2 tablespoons orange juice concentrate, thawed
- 1 tablespoon chopped parsley
- 1 tablespoon lemon juice
- ½ teaspoon dried dillweed
- ½ cup water
- ½ teaspoon salt
- 4 thin orange slices

Preheat broiler. Cut fish into 4 pieces. Place in a shallow pan. Combine orange juice concentrate, parsley, lemon juice, dillweed, water, and salt; mix well; pour over fish. Marinate 30 minutes; turn once. Remove fish from marinade; reserve marinade. Place fish on a broiler pan coated with vegetable spray. Broil for 6 minutes 3 inches from heat. Turn and broil until fish flakes easily, about 5 to 6 minutes. Baste with reserved marinade. Brush marinade on top before serving. Garnish with orange slices.

Lemony Tuna Casserole

Makes 4 servings.
Approximately 172 calories per serving.

- 1 10¾-ounce can cream of celery soup
- ½ teaspoon grated lemon peel
- 1½ tablespoons lemon juice
- 2 6½-ounce cans tuna, packed in water, drained and flaked
- 1 cup cooked peas or leftover vegetable

Preheat oven to 350°. Combine soup, lemon peel, and juice; mix thoroughly. Stir in tuna; add peas and mix lightly. Bake in a lightly greased or nonstick casserole for 20 minutes.

Tartar Sauce

Makes 2 cups.
Approximately 26 calories per ¼-cup serving.

- 1 cup plain low-fat yogurt
- 2 tablespoons chili sauce
- 2 tablespoons chopped dill pickle
- 2 tablespoons chopped onion
- 2 tablespoons chopped green pepper
- 1 tablespoon lemon juice
- ½ teaspoon dry mustard
  Salt and pepper to taste

Combine all ingredients; blend well.

Eggs and Cheese

French Omelet

Makes 6 servings.
Approximately 120 calories per serving.

  6 eggs
¾ teaspoon salt
  Dash black pepper
  1 cup low-fat creamed cottage cheese
¼ cup chopped pimiento
  1 tablespoon margarine

Beat eggs just enough to mix whites and yolks. Add salt, pepper, cottage cheese, and pimiento. Heat margarine in an omelet pan over medium to low heat. Pour a little melted margarine into the beaten eggs; reheat the remainder in the pan. Pour eggs into pan. As mixture cooks on the bottom and sides, prick with a fork so that the egg on top penetrates the cooked surface and runs underneath. When the eggs are almost set, about 10 minutes, fold over, and brown lightly.

Egg Salad Sandwich Filling

Makes 1¼ cups.
Approximately 88 calories per ¼-cup serving.

  4 medium, hard-cooked eggs, finely chopped
  2 tablespoons chopped sweet pickles or pickle relish, drained
¼ cup minced celery or green pepper
  2 tablespoons chopped parsley
  3 tablespoons reduced calorie mayonnaise
¾ teaspoon salt
½ teaspoon dry mustard
  Dash black pepper

Combine chopped eggs, pickles, celery, parsley, and mayonnaise. Season with salt, dry mustard and pepper; mix well.

Carrot Quiche

Makes 6 servings.
Approximately 227 calories per serving.

  2 cups finely shredded carrots
  6 eggs
1¼ cups skim milk
  1 tablespoon instant minced onion
½ teaspoon salt
¼ teaspoon ground ginger
  Dash black pepper
1½ cups shredded Cheddar cheese

Preheat oven to 350°. Bring 1 inch of water to a boil in a medium saucepan. Add carrots; cover and cook until tender, about 5 minutes. Drain thoroughly, pressing out water. Combine eggs, milk, onion, salt, ginger, and pepper in a bowl. Mix until well blended. Combine carrots and cheese in buttered 9-inch quiche dish, stirring to mix. Pour milk mixture over carrots and cheese. Set dish in a large baking pan. Pour very hot water into a baking pan to within ½ inch of top of dish. Bake for 30 to 35 minutes or until knife inserted in center comes out clean. Let stand 5 minutes before serving.

Spinach Soufflé

Makes 6 servings.
Approximately 150 calories per serving.

    Grated Parmesan cheese
  1 10¾-ounce can condensed cream of chicken soup
  1 10-ounce package frozen chopped spinach, cooked and drained
½ cup shredded Cheddar cheese
  1 tablespoon instant minced onion
½ teaspoon crushed marjoram
  6 medium eggs, separated
¼ teaspoon cream of tartar

Preheat oven to 350°. Spray bottom and sides of a 2½-quart soufflé dish or casserole with vegetable coating spray. Dust with Parmesan cheese. In a large saucepan, combine soup, spinach, cheese, onion, and marjoram. Cook, stirring constantly, over medium heat until cheese melts. In a small mixing bowl, beat egg yolks until thick and lemon-colored, about 5 minutes. Blend a small amount of hot soup mixture into yolks. Stir yolk mixture into soup mixture. Beat egg whites and cream of tartar until stiff but not dry and whites no longer slip when bowl is tilted. Gently fold yolk mixture into whites. Carefully pour into prepared dish. For a "top hat" hold spoon upright about 1 inch from the side of the dish and circle mixture to make a ring 1 inch deep. Bake until puffy, delicately browned and soufflé shakes slightly when oven rack is gently moved back and forth, 55 to 60 minutes. Serve immediately.

Golden Egg Salad Casserole

Makes 6 servings.
Approximately 282 calories per serving.

   6 hard-cooked eggs, chopped
   2 tablespoons diced pimiento
   ½ cup diced celery
1½ cups finely crushed soda crackers
   ¼ cup skim milk
   1 cup reduced calorie mayonnaise
   ¼ to ½ teaspoon salt
   ½ teaspoon garlic salt
   ¼ teaspoon black pepper
   1 tablespoon melted margarine

Preheat oven to 400°. Blend eggs, pimiento, celery, 1 cup of the cracker crumbs, milk, mayonnaise, and seasonings. Spread in a shallow, 1-quart casserole or a 9-inch pie plate coated with vegetable spray. Combine remaining cracker crumbs with the margarine. Sprinkle over casserole. Bake until golden brown, about 25 minutes.

Pickled Eggs and Beets

Makes 6 servings.
Approximately 120 calories per serving.

1 16-ounce jar pickled beets
6 medium, hard-cooked eggs, shelled

Drain beets and reserve juice. Place eggs in beet juice. Cover and refrigerate several hours or overnight, turning occasionally to pickle evenly. Drain juice. Cut eggs in half lengthwise.

Spiced Eggs

Makes 12 servings.
Approximately 86 calories per serving.

  2 cups white vinegar
  2 tablespoons sugar
  1 teaspoon salt
  1 medium onion, sliced
  1 teaspoon combined spices: 4 peppercorns,
    1 clove, celery seed, mace, piece of gingerroot or
    packed pickling spice
12 medium, hard-cooked eggs, peeled

Combine vinegar, sugar, salt, sliced onion, and pickling spices; simmer 5 minutes. Place eggs in a 1-quart jar. Pour vinegar mixture over eggs. Cover and refrigerate. (For best flavor, let stand several hours or overnight.) To give additional flavor, add a sprig of dill, a few caraway seeds or a clove of garlic to the pickling liquid. Strips of green and red pepper or carrot add color. Spiced eggs can be refrigerated for up to 2 weeks.

Omelet with Special Mushroom Sauce

Makes 3 servings.
Omelet: Approximately 147 calories per serving.
Sauce: Approximately 119 calories per ⅓-cup serving.

1 tablespoon minced green onion
  Dash crushed tarragon leaves
1 tablespoon margarine
1 10¾-ounce can cream of mushroom soup
⅓ cup skim milk

In a saucepan, sauté onion and tarragon in margarine until onion is tender. Blend in soup and milk. Heat, stirring occasionally.

6 medium eggs
3 tablespoons skim milk
  Dash black pepper

Combine eggs, milk, and pepper; mix lightly. Pour into a large frying pan. Cook slowly. As eggs begin to set, lift slightly to allow uncooked egg to flow underneath. Transfer to a platter; make a shallow cut down the center. Pour on part of the sauce; fold in half. Serve with remaining sauce.

Cottage Cheese Sandwich Spread

Makes 2 cups.
Approximately 40 calories per ¼-cup serving.

1½ cups low-fat creamed cottage cheese
  ½ cup chopped celery
  ½ cup grated carrot
  1 teaspoon grated onion
  ½ teaspoon dillweed

Beat cottage cheese on high speed of mixer until smooth. Stir in celery, carrot, onion and dillweed.

Cheesy Chow Mein

Makes 6 servings.
Approximately 217 calories per serving.
Chow mein noodles extra calories.

2 cups cooked, diced celery
1 6½-ounce can tuna, packed in water, drained
  and flaked
1 tablespoon margarine
1 10¾-ounce can cream of mushroom soup
½ cup skim milk
1 10-ounce package frozen peas
1 cup shredded Cheddar cheese

Preheat oven to 350°. In a large frying pan, combine celery, tuna, margarine, soup, milk, and peas. Cook over low heat for ½ hour, stirring frequently. Add cheese and stir until melted. Serve over chow mein noodles, if desired.

Cottage Cheese Meat Loaf

Makes 9 servings.
Approximately 138 calories per serving.

    1 pound lean ground beef
    1 cup low-fat creamed cottage cheese
    ½ cup quick-cooking rolled oats
    1 egg
    ¼ cup catsup
    2 teaspoons prepared mustard
    2 tablespoons chopped green pepper
    2 tablespoons chopped onion
    1 teaspoon salt
      Dash black pepper
    ⅓ cup grated Parmesan cheese

Preheat oven to 350°. Thoroughly mix all ingredients, except Parmesan cheese. Lightly pack mixture into an 8-inch pan. Bake for 20 minutes. Sprinkle cheese on top. Bake for 10 minutes. Let stand 5 minutes; cut into squares.

Cheese Sauce

Makes 1¾ cups sauce.
Approximately 60 calories per ¼-cup serving.

    1 tablespoon margarine
    4 teaspoons flour
    ¼ teaspoon salt
      Dash black pepper
    1 cup skim milk
    ½ cup shredded, process Swiss cheese
    1 tablespoon lemon juice

Melt margarine in a small saucepan. Blend in flour, salt, and pepper. Add milk; cook and stir until thick and bubbly. Remove from heat. Add cheese and lemon juice; stir until cheese melts.

Cheese and Shrimp Custard

Makes 6 servings.
Approximately 204 calories per serving.

    4 slices white bread, crusts may be trimmed
    5 ounces sharp Cheddar cheese
    1 cup cooked shrimp
    2 eggs, lightly beaten
    1½ cups skim milk
    ⅓ teaspoon salt

Preheat oven to 325°. Cut bread into 1-inch squares. Cut cheese into small cubes. Arrange layers of bread, shrimp, and cheese in a casserole coated with vegetable spray. Combine eggs, milk, and salt. Carefully pour into casserole. Place casserole in a pan of hot water. Bake for 1 hour or until eggs are set.

Cheese 'n' Vegetable Casserole

Makes 6 servings.
Approximately 153 calories per serving.

    1 pound fresh spinach, chopped
    1 cup chopped iceberg lettuce
    1 cup chopped green onion
    ½ cup chopped fresh parsley
    1 cup diced Monterey Jack cheese
    4 eggs, lightly beaten
    2 tablespoons margarine, melted
      Plain yogurt

Preheat oven to 325°. Combine the first 5 ingredients; mix lightly. Add eggs and mix well. Coat a casserole or baking dish with melted margarine. Add vegetable mixture and bake for 1 hour, until top is brown and crisp. Serve topped with a dollop of yogurt.

Noodle Cottage Cheese Scallop

Makes 8 servings.
Approximately 247 calories per serving.

    ¼ cup chopped onion
    ¼ cup chopped green pepper
    2 tablespoons margarine
    2 tablespoons flour
    2 teaspoons salt
    ½ teaspoon celery seed
    2 cups skim milk
    1 pound low-fat creamed cottage cheese
    4 cups wide noodles, cooked according to package directions and drained
      Paprika

Preheat oven to 350°. Sauté onion and green pepper in margarine for 5 minutes. Stir in flour, salt, and celery seed. Slowly add milk; cook until thickened. Fold in cottage cheese. Combine noodles and sauce; pour into a sprayed 2-quart casserole. Sprinkle on paprika. Bake about 45 minutes.

Breads

Welsh Rarebit Bread

Makes 2 loaves.
Approximately 97 calories per thin slice.

    5 to 6 cups flour
    2 packages dry yeast
    2 tablespoons granulated sugar
    2 teaspoons salt
    1 teaspoon dry mustard
      Dash cayenne pepper
 1½ cups skim milk
    ½ cup water
    8 ounces process American cheese, cubed
    2 tablespoons margarine
    1 tablespoon Worcestershire sauce

Stir together 2 cups of the flour, yeast, sugar, salt, mustard, and pepper. Heat milk, water, cheese, and margarine over low heat until cheese is just melted; cool to lukewarm. Add liquids to flour mixture; beat until smooth, about 3 minutes. Stir in Worcestershire sauce. Stir in enough flour to make a soft dough. Turn out onto a floured surface and knead until smooth and elastic, 5 to 8 minutes. Place dough in a greased bowl; turn to grease top. Cover and let rise in a warm place until doubled in bulk. Punch down dough. Divide in half. Roll each half into a 5 x 11-inch rectangle. Cut each rectangle into 3 long strips, leaving strips joined at 1 end. Braid from uncut end. Place in 2 sprayed 8 x 4 x 2-inch loaf pans. Cover and let rise in a warm place until doubled in bulk. Bake in a preheated 350° oven for 45 to 55 minutes or until deep golden brown. Cover with foil, if browning too quickly. Remove from pans and cool on a wire rack.

Sweet Potato Bread

Makes 2 loaves.
Approximately 81 calories per thin slice.

 5½ to 6 cups flour
    2 packages dry yeast
    1 cup skim milk
    ¾ cup water
    1 cup mashed sweet potato
    2 tablespoons vegetable oil
    2 tablespoons granulated sugar
    1 tablespoon salt
      Vegetable oil

Stir together 2 cups of the flour and dry yeast. Heat milk, water, sweet potato, oil, sugar, and salt until very warm (120 to 130°). Pour liquid all at once into flour mixture. Beat at medium speed of an electric mixer until smooth, about 2 minutes. Stir in enough additional flour to make a moderately stiff dough. Turn onto a lightly-floured surface; knead until smooth and elastic, 8 to 10 minutes. Shape into a ball. Cover with bowl; let rest 30 minutes. Divide dough in half. Roll out into 7 x 14-inch rectangles. Roll up jelly-roll fashion from the short side, pressing dough into roll at each turn. Press ends to seal; fold end under loaf. Place in 2 sprayed 8 x 4 x 2-inch loaf pans; brush with oil. Place in a warm place until doubled in bulk, about 45 minutes. Bake in a preheated 400° oven for 35 to 40 minutes. Cover with a foil tent if bread browns too rapidly. Remove from pans and cool on a wire rack.

Dilly Bread

Makes 1 round loaf.
Approximately 72 calories per thin slice.

    1 package dry yeast
    ¼ cup warm water (110 to 115°)
    2 tablespoons sugar
    1 teaspoon salt
    1 cup creamed low-fat cottage cheese, heated
      to lukewarm
    3 tablespoons margarine, melted
    2 tablespoons grated onion
    2 teaspoons dillweed
    1 egg, lightly beaten
    ¼ teaspoon baking soda
 2¼ to 2½ cups flour
      Softened margarine
      Salt

Dissolve yeast in water in a mixing bowl. Stir in sugar and salt. Blend in cottage cheese, 3 tablespoons margarine, onion, dillweed, egg, soda, and half of the flour. Beat until smooth. Stir in enough remaining flour to make a slightly stiff dough. Cover with a damp towel. Let rise in a warm, draft-free place until doubled in bulk, about 1 hour. Stir batter down. Turn into a sprayed 1½-quart round casserole. Cover with greased waxed paper; let rise in a warm place until doubled in bulk, 30 to 40 minutes. Bake at 350° for 40 to 50 minutes or until golden brown. Brush with margarine and sprinkle with salt. Cool slightly on a wire rack. Slice and serve.

Hors d'Oeuvre Bread

Makes 60 1½-inch rolls.
About 50 calories per roll.

5½ to 6 cups flour
  2 tablespoons sugar
  2 teapoons salt
  1 package dry yeast
1½ cups water
  ½ cup skim milk
  3 tablespoons margarine
  1 egg, well beaten
  3 tablespoons water

In a large bowl, combine 2 cups of the flour, sugar, salt, and yeast. Combine water, milk, and margarine in a saucepan. Heat over low heat until liquids are very warm (120 to 130°). Gradually add to dry ingredients; beat 2 minutes at medium speed of an electric mixer, scraping bowl occasionally. Add ¾ cup flour. Beat at high speed for 2 minutes, scraping the bowl occasionally. Stir in enough additional flour to make a soft dough. Turn out onto a lightly floured board; knead until smooth and elastic, about 8 to 10 minutes. Place in a greased bowl; turn to grease top. Cover and let rise in a warm, draft-free place until doubled in bulk, about 1 hour. Punch down dough; turn out onto a lightly floured board. Cover and let rest for 15 minutes. Divide dough into 60 equal pieces. Form each into a small ball. Place a 1½-pint greased bowl on a wire cooling rack covered with greased aluminum foil. Starting at the bottom, place balls in a circle around the bowl until the bowl is completely filled. Cover and let rise in a warm, draft-free place for 1 hour. Combine egg and water. Brush entire surface of bread. Place cooling rack directly on oven rack. Bake at 350° for 30 to 35 minutes, or until golden brown. Remove bowl. Cool on wire rack. If desired, spear meat and cheese chunks on toothpicks; press toothpicks into each roll.

Cheese Stacks

Makes 40 to 50 1½-inch stacks.
Approximately 23 calories each.

  1 cup flour
  ½ teaspoon salt
  ⅓ cup margarine
  3 to 5 tablespoons water
  1 cup grated Cheddar cheese
  1 egg white
    Poppy or caraway seed

Preheat oven to 450°. Sift flour and salt together. Cut in margarine. Gradually add water and stir until pastry holds together. Roll out to ⅛-inch thickness. Spread half of the dough with part of the grated cheese. Fold in half. Roll out again. Spread cheese on half; fold and roll again. Brush top with egg white. Sprinkle with remaining cheese and poppy or caraway seed. Cut out with a biscuit cutter. Bake for 10 to 12 minutes.

No-Knead Bran Bread

Makes 1 loaf.
Approximately 90 calories per thin slice.

  3 cups flour
  ½ cup instant nonfat dry milk powder
1½ teaspoons salt
  2 packages dry yeast
  ¼ cup granulated sugar
1½ cups warm water (110 to 115°)
  2 cups bran cereal
  1 egg
  ⅓ cup margarine, softened

Stir together flour, dry milk, and salt; set aside. Combine yeast, sugar, and warm water in large mixing bowl. Stir in bran cereal. Let stand about 2 minutes, until cereal softens. Add egg, margarine, and about half of the flour mixture. Beat at medium speed of an electric mixer for about 2 minutes. Mix in remaining flour mixture by hand to form a stiff, sticky dough. Cover and let rise in a warm place until doubled in bulk, about 1 hour. Stir down dough to original size. Spoon into a sprayed 9 x 5 x 3-inch loaf pan. Bake in a preheated 375° oven about 45 minutes or until loaf sounds hollow when lightly tapped. Immediately remove from pan and cool on a wire rack.

Rye Batter Bread

Makes 1 loaf.
Approximately 67 calories per thin slice.

  1 package dry yeast
1¼ cups warm water (110 to 115°)
  2 tablespoons light molasses
2½ cups flour
  1 cup rye flour
  2 teaspoons salt
  1 tablespoon caraway seed, optional
  2 tablespoons margarine
    Softened margarine

Dissolve yeast in warm water in a large mixing bowl. Add molasses, 1¼ cups of the flour, ½ cup of the rye flour, salt, caraway seed, and 2 table-spoons margarine. Blend 30 seconds on low speed, scraping the bowl constantly. Beat 2 minutes on medium speed, scraping the bowl occasionally. Stir in remaining flours; beat until smooth. Scrape batter from the side of the bowl. Cover and let rise in a warm place until doubled in bulk, about 30 minutes. Stir down batter. Spread evenly in sprayed 9 x 5 x 3-inch loaf pan. Smooth top of batter by patting with a floured hand. Cover and let rise until batter is 1 inch from the top of the pan, about 30 minutes. Bake in a preheated 375° oven for 45 to 50 minutes or until loaf sounds hollow when tapped. Brush bread with softened margarine. Remove from pan; cool on a wire rack.

Country Egg Bread

Makes 3 loaves.
Approximately 91 calories per thin slice.

1¾ cups skim milk, scalded
½ cup margarine
⅓ cup honey
1 tablespoon salt
3 cups bite-size crispy wheat squares
¼ cup instant potato flakes
½ cup nonfat dry milk
2 packages dry yeast
½ cup warm water (110 to 115°)
4 eggs, at room temperature, lightly beaten
6½ to 7½ cups flour
1 egg white, beaten with 1 tablespoon water

Pour scalded milk into a large mixing bowl. Add margarine, honey, salt, cereal, potato flakes, and dry milk; mix well. Dissolve yeast in warm water. Add to cereal mixture. Beat in eggs. Gradually, add flour, stirring to form a stiff dough. Turn out onto a lightly floured surface and knead until dough is smooth and elastic, about 10 minutes. Place in a greased bowl; turn to grease top. Cover and let rise in a warm place until doubled in bulk, 1 to 1½ hours. Punch down dough. Let rise 30 minutes. Divide into 3 equal pieces. Knead each piece 1 to 2 minutes. Shape into loaves. Place in 3 sprayed 8 x 4 x 2-inch loaf pans. Brush with egg white mixture. Cover and let rise in a warm place until doubled in bulk, about 30 minutes. Preheat oven to 375°. Bake loaves about 30 minutes or until golden brown and loaf sounds hollow when tapped. Remove from pans. Cool on a wire rack.

Quick Onion Bread

Makes 1 loaf.
Approximately 77 calories per thin slice.

1 cup skim milk
1 egg, lightly beaten
¼ cup margarine, melted
1 envelope onion soup mix
3 cups flour
2 tablespoons granulated sugar
1 tablespoon baking powder

Preheat oven to 350°. In a large bowl, blend milk, egg, and margarine. Add soup mix. Add flour, sugar, and baking powder; stir until just blended. Spray a 9 x 5 x 3-inch loaf pan with vegetable coating; place dough in pan. Bake 50 minutes or until bread tests done. Cool for 5 minutes on a wire rack. Remove from pan and cool completely.

Whole Wheat Bread

Makes 1 loaf.
Approximately 94 calories per thin slice.

2 packages dry yeast
¾ cup warm water (110 to 115°)
1¼ cups buttermilk
1½ cups all-purpose flour
3 cups whole wheat flour
¼ cup margarine
2 tablespoons granulated sugar
2 teaspoons baking powder
2 teaspoons salt
Softened margarine

Dissolve yeast in warm water in a large mixing bowl. Add buttermilk, white flour, 1 cup of the whole wheat flour, the ¼ cup margarine, sugar, baking powder, and salt. Blend ½ minute on low speed, scraping bowl constantly. Beat 2 minutes on medium speed, scraping bowl occasionally. Stir in remaining whole wheat flour. Dough should be soft and slightly sticky. Turn dough onto a well-floured board; knead 5 minutes, until smooth and elastic. Roll dough into a 9 x 18-inch rectangle. Roll up from the short side. Press ends to seal; fold ends under loaf. Place, seam-side down, in a sprayed 9 x 5 x 3-inch loaf pan. Brush loaf lightly with margarine. Let rise in a warm place until doubled in bulk, about 1 hour. Center should come about 2 inches above pan. Heat oven to 425°. Bake 30 to 35 minutes or until deep golden brown. Remove loaf from pan. Brush with margarine; cool on a wire rack.

Desserts

Summer Breeze

Makes 6 servings.
Approximately 75 calories per serving.

- 1 teaspoon ground ginger
- ½ cup low-fat whipped topping
- 2 small cantaloupe
- 1 pint strawberries
- ¼ cup flaked or shredded coconut, optional

Stir ginger into 1 tablespoon of the whipped topping; blend into remaining topping. Refrigerate at least 30 minutes to develop flavor. Cut cantaloupe in half crosswise or into 3 pieces lengthwise; remove seeds; reserve shells. Carefully remove pulp; cut into ¾-inch cubes. Wash and hull strawberries, reserving 4 to 6 whole berries for garnish. Cut strawberries in half. Chill all fruit. Just before serving, combine topping mixture, coconut, and fruit; spoon into cantaloupe shells; garnish with whole berries.

Raspberry Velvet Cream

Makes 6 servings.
Approximately 100 calories per serving.

- 2 envelopes unflavored gelatin
- ½ cup cold water
- ½ cup boiling water
- 1 cup skim milk
- 2 teaspoons imitation raspberry or strawberry extract
- 1 pint vanilla ice milk
- 2 tablespoons sugar
- ⅛ teaspoon red food color, optional

Soften gelatin in cold water. Add boiling water; stir to dissolve. In a blender, combine gelatin, milk, extract, ice milk, sugar, and food color; blend until smooth. Pour into 6 serving dishes; chill until set.

Sea-Breeze Dessert

Makes 6 1-cup servings.
Approximately 83 calories per serving.

- 1 cup boiling water
- 1 envelope (4-serving size) low-calorie lime-flavored gelatin
- ⅔ cup cold water
- 3 tablespoons creme de menthe
- ⅓ cup instant nonfat dry milk
- ⅓ cup ice water
- 2 medium bananas, thinly sliced

Pour boiling water over gelatin; stir until dissolved. Stir in cold water and creme de menthe. Chill until mixture thickens slightly. Chill a small bowl and beater. Combine nonfat milk with ice water in the bowl; beat until light and fluffy. Fold into the thickened gelatin and blend well. Fold in bananas. Spoon into individual serving dishes; chill until firm.

Cocoa Delights

Makes 4 to 5 dozen 2-inch cookies.
Approximately 35 calories per cookie.

- ⅓ cup sunflower oil margarine
- ⅓ cup low-fat vanilla yogurt
- ½ cup sugar
- 1 teaspoon vanilla
- 2 cups sifted flour
- 2 teaspoons unsweetened cocoa
- ¼ teaspoon salt
- 1 teaspoon baking powder
- 1 teaspoon cinnamon
- 1 egg white, lightly beaten

Preheat oven to 325°. Cream margarine, yogurt, sugar, and vanilla in a bowl. Sift together flour, cocoa, salt, baking powder, and cinnamon; blend into margarine mixture. Shape dough into a ball; wrap in waxed paper; chill at least 2 hours. Roll out to slightly less than ¼ inch thick. Cut with a 2-inch cookie cutter. Place on an ungreased baking sheet. Brush with egg white. Bake for 15 minutes.

Lime Mint Pie

Makes 6 servings.
Approximately 124 calories per serving.

- 1 envelope (4-serving size) low-calorie, lime-flavored gelatin
- 1 cup boiling water
- ¾ cup cold water
- 1 cup prepared, low-calorie whipped topping
- ¼ teaspoon peppermint extract
- 1 8-inch pie crust, baked and cooled
  Lime slices, optional

Dissolve gelatin in boiling water. Stir in cold water. Chill until slightly thickened. Gradually blend whipped topping into thickened gelatin; stir in extract. Pour into pie shell. Chill until set, about 2 hours. Garnish with lime slices.

Fresh Strawberry Chiffon Dessert

Makes 6 servings.
Approximately 44 calories per ½-cup serving.

- 1 envelope (4-serving size) low-calorie, strawberry-flavored gelatin
- 1 cup boiling water
- 1 pint strawberries, hulled and crushed
- 1 tablespoon lemon juice
- 1 cup prepared, low-calorie whipped topping

Dissolve gelatin in boiling water. Stir in strawberries and lemon juice. Chill until slightly thickened. Fold in whipped topping. Spoon into individual dessert dishes. Chill until set, about 2 hours.

Bavarian Fruit-Nut Ring

Makes 10 servings.
Approximately 114 calories per serving.

- 1 8-ounce can crushed pineapple, in unsweetened juice
- 2 3-ounce packages low-calorie, orange-flavored gelatin
- 2 cups boiling water
- 1 4-ounce container nondairy whipped topping, thawed
- ½ cup chopped walnuts
- 2 small bananas, diced

Drain pineapple; measure juice. Add water to juice to make 1½ cups. Dissolve gelatin in boiling water. Add pineapple liquid. Pour 1 cup into a 6-cup ring mold. Chill until partially set. Chill remaining gelatin until slightly thickened. Fold in whipped topping. Fold in pineapple, nuts, and bananas. Spoon over the gelatin in the mold. Chill until firm, at least 3 hours. Unmold.

Banana Coffee Cream

Makes 6 servings.
Approximately 105 calories per serving.

- 1 whole egg
- 1 egg, separated
- 4 tablespoons sugar, divided
- ¼ teaspoon salt
- 4 teaspoons instant coffee
- 2 cups skim milk
- 1 envelope unflavored gelatin
- ¼ cup cold water
- ½ cup mashed banana
- 1½ teaspoons vanilla

Lightly beat egg and yolk in the top of a double boiler. Combine 3 tablespoons of the sugar, salt, and coffee; stir into the eggs. Stir in milk. Cook over low heat until the mixture begins to thicken, 15 to 20 minutes, stirring constantly. Soften gelatin in cold water, stir into the hot custard. Chill until the mixture begins to thicken. Stir in banana and vanilla; mix well. Beat egg white until soft peaks form. Gradually beat in remaining 1 tablespoon sugar. Fold into egg mixture. Pour into 6 individual molds; chill until firm.

Pineapple Sponge

Makes 8 servings.
Approximately 50 calories per serving.

- 1 envelope unflavored gelatin
- ¼ cup cold water
- 1 cup unsweetened pineapple juice, heated
- 1 tablespoon fresh lemon or lime juice
- ¼ teaspoon salt
- 1½ teaspoons vanilla
- ½ cup crushed pineapple in unsweetened juice, drained
- 2 egg whites
- 2 tablespoons sugar

Soften gelatin in water. Stir in hot pineapple juice, lemon or lime juice, salt, and vanilla. Chill until the mixture is about as thick as unbeaten egg whites. Beat until fluffy with an electric or rotary beater. Fold in crushed pineapple. Beat egg whites until soft peaks form. Gradually beat in sugar. Fold into the gelatin mixture. Turn into a 1-quart mold rinsed in cold water. Chill until firm. Unmold onto a serving plate. Garnish with fresh mint, if desired.

Peppermint Whip

Makes 7 ⅔-cup servings.
Approximately 21 calories per serving.

- 1 envelope (4-serving size) low-calorie lime-flavored gelatin
- 1 cup boiling water
- 1 cup cold water
- ¼ teaspoon peppermint extract
- 1 cup prepared, low-calorie whipped topping

Dissolve gelatin in boiling water. Add cold water and extract. Place bowl of gelatin in a larger bowl of ice water; stir until slightly thickened. Whip until about doubled in volume. Blend in the whipped topping. Spoon into individual dessert dishes. Chill until set, about 1 hour.

Chocolate Cloud

Makes 8 servings.
Approximately 90 calories per serving.

1 envelope unflavored gelatin
⅓ cup sugar
¼ cup unsweetened cocoa
2 eggs, separated
2 cups skim milk
1½ teaspoons vanilla

In a medium saucepan, mix gelatin, sugar, and cocoa; blend in egg yolks beaten with 1 cup of the skim milk. Stir over low heat until gelatin dissolves, about 5 minutes. Add remaining 1 cup milk and vanilla; chill, stirring occasionally, until mixture mounds slightly when dropped from a spoon. In a large bowl, beat egg whites until soft peaks form; gradually add gelatin mixture and beat until mixture doubles in volume, about 5 minutes. Turn into 8 dessert dishes or a 4-cup bowl. Chill until set, about 4 hours.

Pear Snow

Makes 6 servings.
Approximately 84 calories per serving.

2 fresh Bartlett pears
2 tablespoons lemon juice
1½ tablespoons cornstarch
4 tablespoons sugar, divided
3 tablespoons fresh orange juice
2 egg whites

Preheat oven to 450°. Halve, core and chop pears. Combine pears, lemon juice, cornstarch, 3 tablespoons of the sugar, and the orange juice in a saucepan. Stir and cook over medium heat until sauce comes to a boil and thickens. Pour into an 8-inch round baking dish. Chill. Beat egg whites until stiff; beat in remaining 1 tablespoon sugar. Place egg whites over the pear sauce; bake until golden.

Orange-Coconut Angel

Makes 16 servings.
Approximately 115 calories per serving.

1 package angel food cake mix
2 tablespoons grated orange peel
2 tablespoons flaked coconut

Prepare angel food cake mix as directed, folding in the grated orange and coconut with the flour-sugar mixture. Invert tube pan on a funnel; let stand until cake is completely cool.

Lo-Cal Lemon Cheesecake

Makes 12 servings.
Approximately 150 calories per serving.

2 envelopes unflavored gelatin
¾ cup sugar
2 eggs, separated
1½ cups skim milk
1½ tablespoons lemon juice
1½ teaspoons grated lemon peel
3 cups low-fat creamed cottage cheese
⅓ cup graham cracker crumbs
¼ teaspoon ground cinnamon
⅛ teaspoon ground nutmeg

In a medium saucepan, combine the unflavored gelatin and ½ cup of the sugar. Beat egg yolks with 1 cup milk. Add to gelatin. Stir over low heat until gelatin dissolves, about 5 minutes; add remaining ½ cup milk, lemon juice, and peel. In a large bowl, beat cottage cheese until smooth. Gradually add gelatin mixture to cottage cheese; mix well. Chill, stirring occasionally, until mixture mounds slightly when dropped from spoon. In a large bowl, beat egg whites until soft peaks form. Gradually add remaining ¼ cup sugar and beat until stiff. Fold in cheese mixture. Turn into an 8- or 9-inch springform. Mix graham cracker crumbs, cinnamon, and nutmeg. Sprinkle on top of cheesecake. Chill until firm, at least 3 hours.

Fresh Fruit Combo

Makes 8 servings.
Approximately 79 calories per serving.

2 grapefruit, peeled and sectioned
1 large cantaloupe, cut into 1-inch cubes
1 pound grapes (about 2½ cups)
1 cup fresh or frozen blueberries
Orange Cream Dressing

Arrange fruit in a serving bowl; chill. Serve with Orange Cream Dressing.

Orange Cream Dressing

Makes 1 cup.
Approximately 48 calories per tablespoon.

½ cup dairy sour cream
½ cup marshmallow creme
1 tablespoon grated orange peel
2 tablespoons fresh orange juice

Combine all ingredients in a small bowl. Stir until smooth. Chill.

Orange Treats

Makes 4 to 5 dozen 2-inch cookies.
Approximately 35 calories per cookie.

⅓ cup sunflower oil margarine
⅓ cup low-fat vanilla yogurt
½ cup sugar
1 teaspoon vanilla
2 cups sifted flour
¼ teaspoon salt
½ teaspoon baking soda
2 teaspoons grated orange rind
1 egg white, lightly beaten

Preheat oven to 325°. Cream margarine, yogurt, sugar, and vanilla in a bowl. Sift together flour, salt, and soda; add flour mixture and orange rind to margarine mixture; blend until smooth. Shape dough into a ball; wrap in waxed paper and chill at least 2 hours. Roll out ¼ inch thick on a lightly floured board. Cut with a 2-inch cookie cutter; place on ungreased baking sheets. Brush with egg white. Bake for 15 minutes or until golden.

Fresh Orange Yogurt Parfait

Makes 4 servings.
Approximately 105 calories per serving.

1 cup plain low-fat yogurt
1 tablespoon grated orange peel
1 tablespoon honey
1 orange, peeled and cut in bite-size pieces
1 banana, sliced
1 apple, cut into bite-size pieces

In a small bowl, combine yogurt, orange peel, and honey; chill. Layer fruit and yogurt mixture in 4 parfait glasses or serving dishes.

Baked Custard

Makes 6 servings.
Approximately 98 calories per serving.

2 cups skim milk
3 eggs
¼ cup sugar
¼ teaspoon salt
1½ teaspoons vanilla

Preheat oven to 325°. Scald 1¾ cups of the milk over very low heat. In a separate bowl, lightly beat eggs. Blend in sugar, salt, vanilla, and remaining ¼ cup milk. Stir in hot milk. Strain ½ cup into each of 6 custard cups. Place in a pan of hot water. Bake for 45 minutes or until a knife inserted in center comes out clean.

Pumpkin Fluff

Makes 5½ cups or 10 servings.
Approximately 104 calories per serving.

1 3-ounce package low-calorie orange-flavored gelatin
¾ cup boiling water
1 package (4-serving size) vanilla-flavored instant pudding and pie filling
1 cup cold skim milk
¼ teaspoon pumpkin pie spice
1 16-ounce can pumpkin
1 4-ounce container nondairy whipped topping, thawed
Finely chopped nuts, optional

Secure a 2-inch waxed paper collar to a 1-quart soufflé dish. Dissolve gelatin in boiling water; cool. Combine pudding mix with the 1 cup cold milk; beat for 1 minute. Blend in spice and cooled gelatin. Chill until slightly thickened. Beat pudding mixture with an electric mixer until thick and fluffy. Blend in pumpkin; fold in whipped topping. Chill until thickened, if necessary; pour into soufflé dish. Chill until set, about 3 hours. Remove collar from dish. Sprinkle sides of soufflé with chopped nuts.

Spicy Applesauce

Makes 4 cups.
Approximately 115 calories per ½-cup serving.

8 medium apples
⅓ cup water
1 strip lemon or lime peel
1 2-inch piece stick cinnamon
3 allspice berries
8 whole cloves
½ cup sugar, approximately

Core apples. Cut into eighths; do not peel. Combine apples, water, lemon peel, and spices in a saucepan. Simmer about 15 minutes or until apples are tender-soft. Press through a food mill or sieve. Add sugar, 2 tablespoons at a time, tasting after each addition. Chill.

Lower-Calorie Pie Crust

Makes 1 8-inch pie crust for 6 servings.
Approximately 108 calories per serving.

¾ cup graham cracker or zwieback crumbs
2 tablespoons margarine, melted

Preheat oven to 350°. Combine crumbs with margarine; mix well. Press into an 8-inch pie plate. Bake for 8 minutes. Cool thoroughly.

Index

Appetizers
Beef and Pearls, 4
Grapefruit Ham
    Roll-Ups, 4
Miniature Meatballs, 4
Pickled Mushrooms, 5
Vegetable Dip for
    Apples, 4
Vegetable Sticks, 4

Beef
Beef and Mushroom
    Kebabs, 28
Beef Stroganoff, 22
Braised Beef
    Slimmer, 25
Brazilian Rump Roast,
    with Fruit
    Garnish, 22
Broiled Liver
    Kebabs, 25
Brunch Beef
    Soufflé, 29
Caribbean Lime
    Steak, 29
Celery Beef Bake, 22
Cornburger Skillet, 29
Cottage Cheese
    Meat Loaf, 53
Festive Filled
    Grilled Steaks, 28
Flank Steak,
    Marinated, 24
Flank Steak, Sunny, 27
Hash, Texas, 29
Hawaiian Meatballs, 27
Herbed Beef and
    Vegetable Kebabs, 24
Liver, Broiled
    Kebabs, 25
Liver Strips in
    Vegetable Puree, 25
Marinated Flank
    Steak, 24
Meatballs,
    Hawaiian, 27
Meatballs,
    Shanghai, 29
Parsleyed Oven
    Pot Roast, 27
Pepper Steak, 27
Pot Roast, Parsleyed
    Oven, 27
Rump Roast, Brazilian
    with Fruit
    Garnish, 22
Sauerbraten, 24
Shanghai Meatballs, 29
Skewered Steak
    Strips, 28
Steak and Vegetables
    Fuji, 28
Steak, Caribbean
    Lime, 29
Steak, Festive Filled
    Grilled, 28
Steak Strips,
    Skewered, 28
Steak-Vegetable
    Duo, 24
Stuffed Peppers
    Trinidad, 28
Sunny Flank Steak, 27
Swedish Cabbage
    Casserole, 25
Texas Hash, 29

Beverages
Fruited Punch, 5
Niced Tea, 5
Orange Nog, 5
Root Beer Float, 5
Sweetheart Punch, 5
Trim Toddy, 5

Breads
Cheese Stacks, 56
Country Egg Bread, 57
Dilly Bread, 54
Hors d'Oeuvre
    Bread, 56
No-Knead
    Bran Bread, 56
Quick Onion Bread, 57
Rye Batter Bread, 56
Sweet Potato Bread, 54
Welsh Rarebit
    Bread, 54
Whole Wheat
    Bread, 57

Cheese
Cheese and Shrimp
    Custard, 53
Cheese 'n' Vegetable
    Casserole, 53
Cheese Sauce, 53
Cheesy Chow Mein, 52
Cottage Cheese
    Meat Loaf, 53
Cottage Cheese,
    Noodle Scallop, 53
Cottage Cheese
    Sandwich Spread, 52
Noodle Cottage Cheese
    Scallop, 53

Chicken
Apricot Chicken, 32
Baked Mustard
    Chicken, 34
Chicken, Apricot, 32
Chicken Breasts a la
    Citron, 31
Chicken Broccoli
    Casserole, 31
Chicken, Chinese with
    Vegetables, 31
Chicken, Grilled
    "Pickled", 33
Chicken Honolulu, 33
Chicken Imperial, 32
Chicken, Pineapple
    Kebabs, 33
Chicken, Piquant, 34
Chicken Ramekins, 31
Chicken, Ratatouille, 32
Chicken, Roasted
    Feast, 33
Chicken, Skillet
    Orange, 33
Chicken with Fresh
    Tomato-Dill
    Sauce, 34
Chicken,
    Yogurt-Baked, 32
Chinese Chicken with
    Vegetables, 31
Grilled "Pickled"
    Chicken, 33
Pineapple Chicken
    Kebabs, 33
Piquant Chicken, 34
Roasted Chicken
    Feast, 33
Skillet Orange
    Chicken, 33

Yogurt-Baked
    Chicken, 32

Desserts
Baked Custard, 63
Banana Coffee
    Cream, 60
Bavarian Fruit-Nut
    Ring, 60
Chocolate Cloud, 61
Cocoa Delights, 59
Fresh Fruit Combo, 61
Fresh Orange Yogurt
    Parfait, 63
Fresh Strawberry
    Chiffon Dessert, 60
Lime Mint Pie, 59
Low-Cal Lemon
    Cheesecake, 61
Lower-Calorie
    Pie Crust, 63
Orange-Coconut
    Angel, 63
Orange Treats, 63
Pear Snow, 61
Peppermint Whip, 60
Pineapple Sponge, 60
Pumpkin Fluff, 63
Raspberry Velvet
    Cream, 59
Sea-Breeze Dessert, 59
Spicy Applesauce, 63
Summer Breeze, 59

Eggs
Carrot Quiche, 50
Egg Salad Sandwich
    Filling, 50
Eggs, Pickled and
    Beets, 52
Eggs, Spiced, 52
French Omelet, 50
Golden Egg Salad
    Casserole, 52
Omelet, French, 50
Omelet with Special
    Mushroom Sauce, 52
Pickled Eggs and
    Beets, 52
Quiche, Carrot, 50
Soufflé, Spinach, 50
Spiced Eggs, 52
Spinach Soufflé, 50

Lamb
Lamb Burgers, 41
Lamb Casserole,
    Low-Cal, 41
Lamb Chops,
    Teriyaki, 41
Lamb Kebabs, 41
Low-Cal Lamb
    Casserole, 41
Teriyaki Lamb
    Chops, 41

Pork
Coriander Pork
    Chops, 38
Oriental Pork, 38
Pork Chops,
    Coriander, 38
Pork Jambalaya, 38
Pork, Oriental, 38
Pork, Smoked with
    Potato-Kraut, 38
Porkebabs Italienne, 38
Smoked Pork with
    Potato-Kraut, 38

Salad Dressings
Blue Cheese
    Dressing, 17
Creamy Low-Calorie
    Dressing, 16
Creamy Orange
    Dressing, 17
Dessert Salad
    Dressing, 16
Dilly Dressing, 16
Lime Dressing, 16
Lite Horseradish
    Dressing, 17
Lively Lemon French
    Dressing, 17
Low-Calorie Thousand
    Island Dressing, 17
Rosy Italian
    Dressing, 17
Tangy Dressing, 16

Salads
Celery Salad, 11
Chicken Dinner
    Salad, 12
Crisp 'n' Clear
    Orange Salad, 13
Fruit Salad, 16
Fruited Chicken
    Salad, 15
Grapefruit Velvet
    Fluff, 12
Julienne Beef Garden
    Salad, 15
Lettuce and Radish
    Slaw, 13
Lettuce and Tomato
    Salad, 13
Mandarin Peanut
    Mold, 12
Orange and Onion
    Salad, 12
Oriental Chicken
    Salad, 11
Pea Salad, 12
Plum Summery
    Salad, 16
Rock Lobster Vegetable
    Salad, 15
Sardine Salad, 11
Saucy Raspberry
    Apple Mold, 11
Scandinavian Ham
    Salad, 11
Slim Potato Salad, 11
Slimmer's Danish
    Salad, 13
Strawberry-Pear
    Delight, 15
Tomatoes
    Vinaigrette, 15
Tossed Mushroom
    Salad, 12
Trim Tuna Salad, 13
Western Dessert
    Salad, 13

Seafood
Apple Tuna Mousse, 47
Baked Fish Steaks
    a la Crecy, 44
Baked Fish
    Supreme, 44
Baked Orange
    Halibut, 49
Broiled Rock Lobster
    Tails, 48
Broiled Scallops, 45

Confetti Fish Rolls, 43
Eggplant Stuffed with
    Tuna, 47
Fiesta Shrimp and
    Rice, 48
Fish au Poivre, 43
Fish, Baked
    Supreme, 44
Fish Creole, 49
Fish Rolls, Confetti, 43
Fish Steaks, Baked,
    a la Crecy, 44
Fish Steaks
    Emperor, 48
Haddock Almondine, 48
Haddock Elegante, 49
Halibut, Baked
    Orange, 49
Halibut Superb, 49
Lemony Tuna
    Casserole, 49
Lobster Newburg, 45
Lobster Thermidor, 47
Rock Lobster
    Continental, 44
Rock Lobster Tails,
    Broiled, 48
Salmon Rolls, 47
Scallops, Broiled, 45
Seaside Casserole, 45
Shrimp and Rice,
    Fiesta, 48
Shrimp Perfection
    Aspic, 48
Sole, Stuffed
    Supreme, 43
South African
    Rarebit, 45
Stuffed Sole
    Supreme, 43
Tartar Sauce, 49
Tuna Aubergines, 43
Tuna Casserole,
    Lemony, 49
Tuna, Eggplant
    Stuffed, 47
Tuna-Lentil Creole, 44
Tuna Mousse,
    Apple, 47
Tuna Ratatouille, 45

Soups and Stews
Asparagus Soup, 6
Beef and Celery
    Stew, 9
Camper's Stew, 8
Chicken and Vegetable
    Stew, 9
Double Mushroom and
    Beef Stew, 9
Fish Stew, 8
Garden Ring Soup, 6
Hamburger Soup, 6
Mulligan Stew, 9
Penny-Pinching Pot, 6
Sauerkraut Soup, 8
Tropical Soup, 6
Tuna Stew, 8
Vegetable Stew, 8

Turkey
Chinese Broiled Turkey
    Steaks, 36
Curried Pineapple
    Turkey Breast
    Roast, 36
Lemon-Barbecued
    Turkey, 34

Mandarin Turkey
    Wings, 36
Salad on a Turkey
    Sandwich, 34
Skillet Turkey Cutlets
    Parmesan, 37
Sweet and Sour Turkey
    Drums, 37
Turkey Breast Roast,
    Curried Pineapple, 3
Turkey Bunwiches, 36
Turkey Chow Mein, 37
Turkey Corn
    Pudding, 37
Turkey Drums, Sweet
    and Sour, 37
Turkey,
    Lemon-Barbecued, 3
Turkey Steaks,
    Chinese-Broiled, 36
Turkey Wings,
    Mandarin, 36

Veal
Veal and Spinach
    Rolls, 40
Veal Delight, 40
Veal Italian, 40
Veal-Olive Birds, 40

Vegetables
Asparagus, Stir-Fried,
    a la Lemon, 18
Baked Fries, 20
Beet-Onion
    Supreme, 20
Braised Cucumbers, 20
Broccoli with
    Sunshine Sauce, 18
Cabbage, Lemon, 20
Carrot-Celery
    Medley, 18
Corn Delight, 21
Creamed Green Beans
    and Mushrooms, 21
Cucumbers, Braised, 20
Deviled Tomatoes, 20
Evergreen Zucchini, 20
German-Style
    Green Beans, 21
Green Beans and
    Mushrooms,
    Creamed, 21
Green Beans,
    German-Style, 21
Lemon Cabbage, 20
Nectarines and
    Tomatoes, 18
Onion, Beet
    Supreme, 20
Peas a la
    Sesame, 21
Stir-Fried Asparagus
    a la Lemon, 18
Tomatoes, Deviled, 20
Zucchini, Evergreen, 20
Zucchini Gondolas, 18

B
C
D
E
F
G
H
J
K
L
M